VOCABULARY
SUCCESS STAGE I

IVY LEAGUE

Icon English Ivy League Vocabulary Success
Stage I

Copyright © 2019 by Icon English Institute

No part of this publication may be reproduced, distributed, or transmitted in any form or by any means, including photocopying, recording, or other electronic or mechanical methods, without the prior written permission of the author, except in the case of brief quotations embodied in critical reviews and certai other non-commercial uses permitted by copyright law.

Icon English
www.iconenglish.com

TABLE OF CONTENTS

Stage One A

- Lesson One 10
- Lesson Two 12
- Lesson Three 14
- Lesson Four 16
- Lesson Five 18
- Lesson Six 20
- Lesson Seven 22
- Lesson Eight 24
- Lesson Nine 26
- Lesson Ten 28
- Lesson Eleven 30
- Lesson Twelve 32
- Lesson Thirteen 34
- Lesson Fourteen 36
- Lesson Fifteen 38
- Lesson Sixteen 40
- Lesson Seventeen 42
- Lesson Eighteen 44
- Lesson Nineteen 46
- Lesson Twenty 48
- Lesson Twenty one 50
- Lesson Twenty two 52
- Lesson Twenty three 54
- Lesson Twenty four 56
- Lesson Twenty five 57
- Lesson Twenty six 60
- Lesson Twenty seven 62
- Lesson Twenty eight 64
- Lesson Twenty nine 66
- Lesson Thirty 68
- Lesson Thirty one 70
- Lesson Thirty two 72
- Lesson Thirty three 74
- Lesson Thirty four 76
- Lesson Thirty five 78

TABLE OF CONTENTS

Stage One B

- Lesson One 82
- Lesson Two 84
- Lesson Three 86
- Lesson Four 88
- Lesson Five 90
- Lesson Six 92
- Lesson Seven 94
- Lesson Eight 96
- Lesson Nine 98
- Lesson Ten 100
- Lesson Eleven 102
- Lesson Twelve 104
- Lesson Thirteen 106
- Lesson Fourteen 108
- Lesson Fifteen 110
- Lesson Sixteen 112
- Lesson Seventeen 114
- Lesson Eighteen 116
- Lesson Nineteen 118
- Lesson Twenty 120
- Lesson Twenty one 122
- Lesson Twenty two 124
- Lesson Twenty three 126
- Lesson Twenty four 128
- Lesson Twenty five 130
- Lesson Twenty six 132
- Lesson Twenty seven 134
- Lesson Twenty eight 136
- Lesson Twenty nine 138
- Lesson Thirty 140
- Lesson Thirty one 142
- Lesson Thirty two 144
- Lesson Thirty three 146
- Lesson Thirty four 148
- Lesson Thirty five 150

INTRODUCTION

Icon English Ivy League Vocabulary Success is a series of books, each of which is intended for you to use when learning English. What's great about our books is that they can be used either with a teacher in a classroom setting or independently in your own time.

Vocabulary is one of the most vital aspects of learning a language. Without a rich vocabulary, how do you express the things you want to say? Furthermore, many students will find that having a vast lexicon can be a huge help when taking exams or writing essays for school. And, though some words may not be used in everyday conversations, less common words are still important to learn for certain assignments or standardized tests. Language is varied and complex. Your vocabulary should be that way too.

To keep things simple, each lesson is comprised of ten words. Their meanings, forms and parts of speech need your full attention so that you can learn how to determine which word in what form works best in which fill-in-the-blank sentence. After the sentences, you will read a passage. These passages contain the same ten words from your vocabulary lesson. Reading these words in a narrative context will help you understand how these words are used, and how you can apply them yourself.

WHO IS THIS SERIES AIMED AT?

STAGE ZERO:
BASIC

Stage Zero begins with a "dead word" and a word list. We call words like happy, tired, or pretty "dead" because they are so overused that their meanings fall flat. Included beneath each "dead word" are other, more complicated words with similar meanings. Stage Zero will help you precisely express what you're trying to say without resorting to stale language. Each word list is sorted into categories so that you can really concentrate your language and distinguish yourself for excellent diction whenever you speak or write in English.

STAGE I:
INTERMEDIATE

After completing Stage Zero, you will have absorbed many intriguing new words. However, Stage I is different. These lessons are aimed at high school students who want to improve their writing skills. Many high school assignments require students to analyze complicated works of literature, but how can you complete those difficult assignments if you can't comprehend the words being used? Stage I will help you discover new, complicated words that you will come across in your classes. Boost your essay marks by completing Stage I!

STAGE II:
ADVANCED

Stage II covers some of the complex words in the English language. Much like Stage I, Stage II will provide you with a word list (plus their part of speech and meaning), fill-in-the-blank sentences, and a short passage. The words in Stage II were chosen by combing through SAT tests from the past few years and picking out the most common words used. However, even if you don't plan on taking the SAT's or ACT's, Stage II is still a vital part of helping you become a fluent speaker and writer of English! Take your skills to the next level and conquer Stage II!

STAGE III:
MASTERY

Stage 3 covers 500 most complex words in the English language. Much like Stage II, Stage III will provide you with a word list (plus their part of speech and meaning), fill-in-the-blank sentences, and a short passage. The words in Stage III were chosen by combing through standardised exams like AP English, ACT, and SAT tests from the past few years and picking out the most challenging words used. However, even if you don't plan on taking any standardised exam like the SAT's or ACT's, Stage III is still a vital part of improving your reading comprehension and enhancing your writing skills!

LESSON ONE

Target Words

1. Abide
2. Ablaze
3. Abolish
4. Acclaimed
5. Accountability
6. Accustom
7. Acknowledge
8. Affection
9. Affectionate
10. Anticipation

LESSON ONE

A. Dictation

____ /10

B. Fill in the blanks with the most appropriate words

01 The recent tax reforms have made the government more _____ for its spending.

02 Do not think that I have come to _____ the law or the prophets. I have come to fulfill them.

03 His father's generosity to him had created a strong and sincere _____ for him in the heart, an _____ without any reservation.

04 He shivered, feeling a muffled _____ and elation.

05 Come what might, he would not bow down or submit or _____ a master. He had no master in death.

06 Anna was rather troubled by the strongly intimate, _____ way her father had towards this young man.

07 A good traveler can _____ himself to almost any kind of food.

08 Penicillin was _____ as the most important discovery during the 1940's.

09 He had never seen the house like this, _____ with light and noisy with voices.

10 I can't _____ to see such cruelty.

LESSON TWO

Target Words

1. Appall
2. Appeal
3. Awkward
4. Barren
5. Belligerent
6. Boundary
7. Brittle
8. Burial
9. Cargo
10. Caution

LESSON TWO

A. Dictation

_____ /10

B. Fill in the blanks with the most appropriate words

01 Churchill looked _____ for a moment, and then swallowed his pride.

02 As to the task of disposing of the bodies, people would choose those _____ methods with which they are most comfortable.

03 Electronic publishing is blurring the _____ between dictionaries and encyclopaedias.

04 I think what _____ to me about his paintings is the colours he uses.

05 Cynics are only happy in making the world as _____ to others as they have made it for themselves.

06 After an _____ pause, the couple returned to the rest of the family and sat.

07 _____with excessive frost, many colossal tough-grained maples, snapped in twain like pipestems, cumbered the unfeeling earth.

08 The newspaper _____ its readers against buying shares without getting good advice first.

09 The boat calls at the main port to load its regular _____ of bananas.

10 Prisoners were kept in the most _____ conditions.

LESSON THREE

Target Words

1. Cautious
2. Clumsiness
3. Clumsy
4. Controversial
5. Coincidental
6. Commodity
7. Commonplace
8. Complexity
9. Conscience
10. Contentment

LESSON THREE

A. Dictation

____ /10

B. Fill in the blanks with the most appropriate words

01 The sheer _____ of the ploy made it sure to be uncovered.

02 Countries have continued to stack up debts because falling prices of _____ like coffee have cut into export earnings.

03 She will be asked to find a solution over the _____ issue of a ban on hunting with dogs.

04 Firms have been unusually _____ about hiring new workers.

05 But left-handers are renowned for being awkward and _____ and in some societies they are still looked upon with suspicion.

06 And isn't it strangely _____ that Scotland Yard were involved in all this, at this particular time?

07 Her faith was a central part of her long life and through it she found much peace, strength and _____.

08 The whole legal system would collapse if even just a few lawyers begin to let their own moral _____ influence their work.

09 Don't let the _____ of the system discourage you from the entire idea.

10 The talent of the comic is to make _____ events remarkable.

LESSON FOUR

Target Words

1. Context
2. Cynical
3. Deceit
4. Decoration
5. Defy
6. Denial
7. Denote
8. Dependent
9. Deter
10. Determination

LESSON FOUR

A. Dictation

____ /10

B. Fill in the blanks with the most appropriate words

01 A few workers have _____ the majority decision and gone into work despite the strike.

02 Mike is such a/an _____ person because he believes that people always act selfishly.

03 The _____ and furnishings had to be practical enough for a family home.

04 There was a message waiting, _____ that someone had been here ahead of her.

05 These measures are designed to _____ an enemy attack.

06 It is very easy to become _____ on sleeping pills.

07 A man who has a great _____ to succeed will never fail.

08 Officials did not believe the runner's _____ that he had taken drugs.

09 She got them to hand over all their money by a wicked _____.

10 It is important to see all the fighting and bloodshed in his plays in historical _____.

LESSON FIVE

Target Words

1. Discard
2. Distracted
3. Discreet
4. Diverse
5. Down-to-earth
6. Drift
7. Easy-going
8. Egotism
9. Embarrassment
10. Endure

LESSON FIVE

A. Dictation

_____ /10

B. Fill in the blanks with the most appropriate words

01 David seems to be a friendly, _____ type of guy, but he can be quite aggressive from time to time.

02 Janice is a/an _____ sort of woman with no pretensions at all.

03 Susan and Deborah share an intensely selfish, _____ streak.

04 The talk _____ aimlessly from one subject to another.

05 New York is a very culturally and ethnically _____ city.

06 Gill seems rather _____ at the moment- I think she's worried about her exams.

07 _____ food containers and bottles littered the streets.

08 The family made _____ enquiries about this young man's background.

09 I shall be left with many _____ memories of the time I spent with her in England.

10 You have been a/an _____ to us from the day Douglas married you.

LESSON SIX

Target Words

1. Energize
2. Eternity
3. Ethical
4. Exhilaration
5. Faith
6. Flourish
7. Forgery
8. Fragrance
9. Frustration
10. Gentleness

LESSON SIX

A. Dictation

_____ /10

B. Fill in the blanks with the most appropriate words

01 Exploiting the workers in developing countries is never a/an _____ investment scheme.

02 The plant _____ particularly well in slightly harsher climes.

03 I laughed out loud in sheer pleasure, feeling the _____ of the contest rush through me.

04 Martin Luther King _____ and mobilized millions of people around the nation with his speeches.

05 One year is not a long time for anyone, but it is a/an _____ for the very young.

06 He thought he would never been found guilty of _____, so he wrote his father's will himself.

07 The mildness and _____ of the February sun is compared to a mother's scolding.

08 This miserable job has more than its fair share of _____.

09 After the trial, his family had lost all _____ in the judicial system.

10 Lavender has a delicate _____.

LESSON SEVEN

Target Words

1. Giggle
2. Guile
3. Harsh
4. Harvest
5. Hatred
6. Highlight
7. Hoarse
8. Insight
9. Icicle
10. Idolize

LESSON SEVEN

A. Dictation

____ /10

B. Fill in the blanks with the most appropriate words

01 When _____ hung from the roof, I knew winter came.

02 What is very clear in these letters is Clark's _____ of his selfish father.

03 A/An _____ upbringing does not necessarily ruin children; instead, it toughens them.

04 The report _____ the need for improved safety in school.

05 The machine gun _____ hundreds of young men's blood every time it roared.

06 The teacher caught Roz _____ over some of Janet's awful poetry homework.

07 The president will need to use all his political _____ to stay in power.

08 She _____ her artist mother, who is as strong and dangerous as she is beautiful.

09 Angela's voice was _____, and barely about a whisper as she reached out her hand to us.

10 She did not seem to have enough _____ into the reasons for this disconnection.

LESSON EIGHT

Target Words

1. Immerse
2. Inspiration
3. Intense
4. Isolate
5. Justified
6. Materialistic
7. Merchandise
8. Mischievous
9. Misinterpret
10. Mistrust

LESSON EIGHT

A. Dictation

_____ /10

B. Fill in the blanks with the most appropriate words

01 I did not realise the _____ of people's feelings on this issue.

02 He _____ himself totally in his work.

03 Several villages have been _____ by heavy snowfalls.

04 The golden autumn light provided the _____ for the painting.

05 The _____ on display in the shop window does not appeal to me at all.

06 She has a deep _____ of anything new or strange.

07 He wrote a book about the _____ antics of his ten-year-old daughter.

08 Have we all become a self-centred society, preoccupied with _____?

09 When we re-examined his report, we realised that we had _____ him.

10 It can be said, with some _____, that she is one of the greatest actresses on the English stage today.

LESSON NINE

Target Words

1. Numb
2. Nuisance
3. Obscene
4. Observe
5. Optimism
6. Outcome
7. Outdated
8. Outlook
9. Palatable
10. Pale

LESSON NINE

A. Dictation

____ /10

B. Fill in the blanks with the most appropriate words

01 He could be a bit of _____ when he was drunk.

02 There was a note of _____ in his voice as he spoke about the company's future.

03 When he was elected to be president, the _____ for the economy was bleak.

04 When someone you love is gone, everything else _____ in comparison.

05 Her ideas on education are rather _____ now.

06 He spent a year in the jungle, _____ how deforestation is affecting local tribes.

07 She was completely _____ by the shock of her father's death.

08 Such deliberate destruction of the environment is a/an _____.

09 It is still too early to predict the _____ of the meeting.

10 Everyone says they want the truth, but the truth is not always _____.

LESSON TEN

Target Words

1. Pessimism
2. Practicality
3. Predominant
4. Prejudice
5. Prematurely
6. Preserve
7. Progressive
8. Prospect
9. Recognize
10. Recollect

LESSON TEN

A. Dictation

_____ /10

B. Fill in the blanks with the most appropriate words

01 There is now a mood of deepening _____ over the economy.

02 The war and the years in the harsh mountains had _____ aged him.

03 The international community has refused to _____ the newly independent nation state.

04 I need to get out of the house from time to time just to _____ my sanity.

05 There is a _____ of men in the hunters club.

06 Decisions about your children should be based on the _____ of everyday life.

07 There's not much _____ that this war will be over soon.

08 I have many pleasant _____ of the time we spent together.

09 There's been a _____ decline in the standard of living over the past few years.

10 Laws against racial _____ must be strictly enforced.

LESSON ELEVEN

Target Words

1. Reckless
2. Reel
3. Reflection
4. Refurbish
5. Relive
6. Reluctant
7. Respected
8. Respectful
9. Reverence
10. Rewarding

LESSON ELEVEN

A. Dictation

_____ /10

B. Fill in the blanks with the most appropriate words

01 Camilla was standing at a _____ distance, looking at the prince.

02 Whenever I smell burning, I _____ the final moments of the car crash.

03 Textbook writing can be an intellectually and financially _____ activity.

04 Many parents feel _____ to talk openly with their children.

05 In Greek mythology, Narcissus fell in love with his own _____ in a pool water.

06 He is charged with causing death by _____ driving.

07 The angler _____ the trout in slowly.

08 Today, we cannot even trust the country's most _____ daily newspaper.

09 The house will be _____ for the new tenants.

10 Nelson Mandela is _____ for his brave fight against apartheid.

LESSON TWELVE

Target Words

1. Ritual
2. Rub
3. Run-down
4. Rustle
5. Scent
6. Scrap
7. Selfish
8. Self-sufficient
9. Shabby
10. Shatter

LESSON TWELVE

A. Dictation

____ /10

B. Fill in the blanks with the most appropriate words

01. The book _____ all her illusions about the Romans.

02. Her home is a rented one-bedroom apartment in a _____ part of town.

03. I've read every _____ of information I can find on the subject.

04. There are always times when you are feeling tired and _____.

05. Coffee and the newspaper are part of my morning _____.

06. She yawned and _____ her eyes sleepily.

07. He _____ his papers to hide his embarrassment.

08. Cabinet Ministers are _____ pursuing their own vested interests.

09. The air was _____ with roses.

10. The programme aims to make the country _____ in food production and to cut energy imports.

LESSON THIRTEEN

Target Words

1. Solitude
2. Spite
3. Split
4. Spontaneity
5. Stiff
6. Still
7. Strict
8. Suspenseful
9. Thrill
10. Timeless

LESSON THIRTEEN

A. Dictation

____ /10

B. Fill in the blanks with the most appropriate words

01 After months of _____ at sea, it felt strange to be in company.

02 His jokes seemed _____, but were in fact carefully prepared beforehand.

03 He tried to _____ the baby's cries by cuddling her.

04 It gave me a real _____ to see her again after so many years.

05 The city has a _____ quality as if it had existed forever.

06 A _____ curfew has been imposed from dusk till dawn.

07 Mary mixed the powder and water into a _____ paste.

08 David's the sort of man who would let down the tires on your car just out of _____.

09 The _____ and sinister tale made me feel so anxious about what was going to happen in the story next.

10 She _____ the aubergines in half and covered with breadcrumbs.

LESSON FOURTEEN

Target Words

1. Tolerance
2. Trivia
3. Trot
4. Triumph
5. Uninviting
6. Unique
7. Unmanageable
8. Upbringing
9. Ubiquitous
10. Ultimate

LESSON FOURTEEN

A. Dictation

____ /10

B. Fill in the blanks with the most appropriate words

01. The _____ luxury of the trip was flying in Concorde.

02. Indulged children tend to become _____ when they reach their teens.

03. The signing of the agreement was a personal _____ for the Prime Minster.

04. Some would like to see it develop a greater _____ of contrary points of view in this country.

05. Sexual harassment in the workplace is not a _____ matter.

06. The hotel room was bare and _____.

07. Is it right to say all the crimes he committed were simply the result of his _____?

08. The radio, that most _____ of consumer-electronic appliances, is about to enter a new age.

09. Each person's genetic code is _____ except in the case of identical twins.

10. Although she retired from politics five years ago, she still _____ around the globe, giving speeches and meeting world leaders.

LESSON FIFTEEN

Target Words

1. Accepting
2. Accommodating
3. Admiring
4. Adoring
5. Affluent
6. Ambitious
7. Ambivalent
8. Amused
9. Antagonistic
10. Apathetic

LESSON FIFTEEN

A. Dictation

____ /10

B. Fill in the blanks with the most appropriate words

01 Nearly all the women I interviewed were aggressively _____ towards the idea that women should stay at home.

02 The government has announced a/an _____ program to modernize the railway network throughout the country.

03 Annette was getting lots of _____ glances in her new red dress.

04 She was always more _____ of coaching suggestions than direct orders.

05 Dianna agreed to marry Jack but refused to play the part of the _____ wife.

06 I have never lied about my feelings, including my _____ about getting married with my best friend's wife after he passed away.

07 Don't be so _____. How are you going to get a job if you don't even care about your resume?

08 Sara was not _____ by Franklin's teasing at all; she was quite offended.

09 The postwar era was one of new _____ for the working class in the US.

10 I'm sure Janice will help you – she is always very _____ whenever someone needs her aid.

LESSON SIXTEEN

Target Words

1. Apologetic
2. Apprehensive
3. Appreciative
4. Argumentative
5. Arrogant
6. Assertive
7. Athletic
8. Benevolent
9. Bewildered
10. Bitter

LESSON SIXTEEN

A. Dictation

____ /10

B. Fill in the blanks with the most appropriate words

01 The law students share a/an _____ attitude toward political issues.

02 Jenny is physically strong, healthy and active, so she looks very _____.

03 He was a/an _____ old man, who wouldn't even hurt a fly.

04 She'd suffered terribly over the years, but it hadn't made her _____ about her life here.

05 I've invited a lot of people to my birthday party, but I'm a bit _____ that no one will show up.

06 I'm very _____ of all the support you have given me.

07 Arriving in a strange city at night, I felt alone and _____ by the noise and neon lights outside my hotel room.

08 It is _____ of you to assume you will win every time.

09 If you really want the promotion, you will have to state your opinions in a/an _____ tone of voice.

10 The hospital staff were very _____ about forgetting her pills, but that couldn't really compensate for her sufferings.

LESSON SEVENTEEN

Target Words

1. Bold
2. Captivating
3. Callous
4. Candid
5. Caustic
6. Cautionary
7. Celebratory
8. Chaotic
9. Charitable
10. Cheerful

LESSON SEVENTEEN

A. Dictation

____/10

B. Fill in the blanks with the most appropriate words

01 Her _____ smile and alluring looks easily fascinated her audience.

02 He is a _____ sort of a person – always trying to do twenty things at once.

03 He walked in, _____ as brass, and asked me to lend him 50 bucks.

04 A _____ man giving much money to feed the poor is sometimes reluctant to help his own family members.

05 She's well-known in the office for her _____ wit, which hurts a lot of co-workers' feelings.

06 Let me be quite _____ with you: your work is not good enough.

07 When we heard she'd got the job, we all went off for a _____ drink.

08 Thomas made up his mind to go to Nigeria despite his father's _____ advice.

09 The doctor's waiting room was bright and _____ with yellow walls and curtains.

10 It might sound _____, but I don't really care if he is broke. He is not my family.

LESSON EIGHTEEN

Target Words

1. Compassionate
2. Complacent
3. Compliant
4. Complimentary
5. Conceited
6. Condescending
7. Congenial
8. Contemptuous
9. Contented
10. Conventional

LESSON EIGHTEEN

A. Dictation

____ /10

B. Fill in the blanks with the most appropriate words

01 Peter, _____ as ever, gave in to any of his manager's demands.

02 We often get _____ remarks regarding the cleanliness of our patio.

03 I enjoy talking to different customers every day because I find this aspect of my job particularly _____.

04 They defied _____ by giving up their regular jobs and becoming self-sufficient.

05 We learn to be _____ and to consider those whose needs are very different to our own.

06 She resented the older neighbours' _____ attitude because they always spoke to her in a patronizing manner.

07 David is such a cynical person that he will not be _____ until he has upset everyone in the office.

08 What really annoys me about them is their _____ - they seem to have no desire to expand their horizons.

09 At school Irene had complete _____ for all her teachers, whom she described as having no real skills.

10 I thought him _____ and arrogant because he was far too proud of his abilities.

LESSON NINETEEN

Target Words

1. Courageous
2. Crooked
3. Crucial
4. Demeaning
5. Depressing
6. Despairing
7. Detached
8. Dignified
9. Diplomatic
10. Disapproving

LESSON NINETEEN

A. Dictation

____/10

B. Fill in the blanks with the most appropriate words

01 Getting this contract is _____ to the future of our company.

02 Polly gave her a _____ smile, a broad grin that amused her.

03 The defeated candidate who run for president gave a _____ speech in which he congratulated his rival.

04 Sophie rubbed her _____ hands over her face, knowing that everything was wrong and nothing would turn out well.

05 It was _____ of her to challenge the managing director's unwise decision.

06 He found it _____ to have to work for his high school classmate who once stole his girlfriend from his arms.

07 He tried to remain emotionally _____ from the prisoners, but the excitement in his voice betrayed him.

08 You can be polite, politic and _____, or you can be blunt and honest.

09 Hearing Mary's absurd proposal, Marcus shot a _____ glance at her.

10 It is quite _____ to think that most of us live no more than 30000 days.

LESSON TWENTY

Target Words

1. Disenfranchised
2. Disparaging
3. Distressing
4. Disdained
5. Distraught
6. Disheartened
7. Defeatist
8. Desolate
9. Depressive
10. Determined

LESSON TWENTY

A. Dictation

____ /10

B. Fill in the blanks with the most appropriate words

01 David was very _____ by the result of the test; he failed the road test again.

02 Mary's _____ remarks on Joseph's efforts were obviously out of jealousy.

03 Throughout the postwar era, desperate and _____ young people in developing countries sought solace in communism.

04 The older musicians _____ the new, rock-influenced music.

05 A _____ is someone who thinks or talks in a way that suggests that they expect to be unsuccessful.

06 The missing child's _____ parents made an appeal for information on TV.

07 The television reports about the famine were particularly _____.

08 Staying in the empty room, we all felt absolutely _____ when she left us.

09 Peter seems so _____ to get this piece of work finished today, but I know he will be procrastinating again.

10 Tiredness, loss of appetite and sleeping problems are all symptoms of _____.

LESSON TWENTY-ONE

Target Words

1. Docile
2. Earnest
3. Elated
4. Embarrassed
5. Empathetic
6. Empower
7. Empirical
8. Enchant
9. Engaged
10. Enraged

LESSON TWENTY-ONE

A. Dictation

____/10

B. Fill in the blanks with the most appropriate words

01 Although there is no theory to explain it, _____ studies show that some forms of alternative medicine are extremely effective.

02 A little bit of _____ with and sympathy for those unfortunate people might go a long way in making their life easier.

03 When he said he hated all forms of government, I thought he was joking – I did not realize he was in deadly _____.

04 Mary is always ready and willing to be trained, and she is my most _____ horse.

05 She was filled with _____ when her daughter was born.

06 For most teenagers, learning to drive is a/an _____ experience.

07 The _____ light patterns of the Festival of Lights at VanDusen Botanical.

08 Angry words turned to blows, and the _____ Willard drew his pistol and shot the man dead.

09 I called her last night, but her telephone line was _____. Obviously, she was talking to someone else.

10 She felt _____ about undressing in front of the doctor.

LESSON TWENTY-TWO

Target Words

1. Enthusiasm
2. Entreating
3. Envious
4. Euphoric
5. Evasive
6. Exasperate
7. Fascinate
8. Fatalistic
9. Fearsome
10. Feasible

LESSON TWENTY-TWO

A. Dictation

____ /10

B. Fill in the blanks with the most appropriate words

01 One of the good things about teaching is to share children's _____ for learning.

02 She left that first yoga session feeling exhilarated, even _____, and filled with energy and elation.

03 I was _____ to hear about his travels in Bhutan, a country unknown to us.

04 She questioned whether it was _____ to stimulate investment in these regions where the average household income was slightly over $ 10,000 a year.

05 People today are surprisingly more _____ about what's going to happen to themselves than those of the 1930's who believed they could change or control their lives.

06 Michael was such an ill-mannered person, and he had developed a _____ reputation for intimidating people.

07 David was being _____ about his first meeting with the new dean; he must be deliberately hiding something from us.

08 He looked at her so _____, so sure that she would agree to marry him.

09 It is _____ to run for a train and then miss it by half a minute.

10 I'm so _____ of you getting an extra day's holiday.

LESSON TWENTY-THREE

Target Words

1. Finicky
2. Forceful
3. Frank
4. Frivolous
5. Grateful
6. Grim
7. Gullible
8. High-spirited
9. Hostile
10. Humble

LESSON TWENTY-THREE

A. Dictation

____ /10

B. Fill in the blanks with the most appropriate words

01 He must have been pretty _____ to fall for that old trick.

02 Even when Jason turned 18, he was still rather _____ and needed to grow up.

03 Success in business comes not by understanding and meeting the demands of millions of _____ customers, but by cementing relationships with and winning the support of them.

04 To be perfectly _____ with you, I don't think she's the woman for the job.

05 More than 6,000 people took to the streets of Dublin at the weekend in a _____ and colourful celebration.

06 In my _____ opinion, we should never have bought that villa in the first place, my lord.

07 The _____ weather conditions made the mission extremely difficult.

08 We face the _____ prospect of still high unemployment.

09 I would be most _____ if you would send me the book immediately.

10 The opposition leader led a very _____ attack on the government in parliament this morning.

LESSON TWENTY-FOUR

Target Words

1. Humourous (US Humorous)
2. Hypercritical
3. Impatient
4. Impartial
5. Implore
6. Incredulous
7. Indecisive
8. Indeterminate
9. Indifferent
10. Indignant

LESSON TWENTY-FOUR

A. Dictation

____ /10

B. Fill in the blanks with the most appropriate words

01 He became very _____ when it was suggested he had made a mistake.

02 The mayor was criticized as a weak and _____ leader.

03 The state must ensure the independence and _____ of the justice system.

04 David was wrestling with a door, looking _____ at his friends.

05 He's a good trainer, but inclined to be a bit _____ with slow learners.

06 He was a talented man, yet _____ of small faults that won't worry me.

07 Tracy _____ her parents not to send her away to the school in Prince George. The _____ look in her eyes eventually convinced her parents.

08 When Jerry told his parents that he had been admitted to Harvard, his parents' _____ gaze told him that they did not really believe it.

09 She was wearing a coat of a/an _____ pinkish, orangish, reddish colour that I will call 'hot salmon'.

10 The biggest problem awaiting us to solve today is how we have become a society uncaring and _____ to one another.

LESSON TWENTY-FIVE

Target Words

1. Inexorable
2. Informative
3. Insane
4. Insecure
5. Inspired
6. Intellectual
7. Intimate
8. Intimidate
9. Intangible
10. Intrigued

LESSON TWENTY-FIVE

A. Dictation

____/10

B. Fill in the blanks with the most appropriate words

01 Is the _____ progress of science a blessing or a curse?

02 Her husband makes five thousand pounds a year; she feels very _____ about her marriage.

03 Looking after a baby at home all day is nice, but it doesn't provide much _____ stimulation.

04 They were _____ into accepting a pay cut by the threat of losing their jobs.

05 I couldn't tell you why I feel so, but the old building has a/an _____ air of sadness about it.

06 It is a very interesting story, and I'm _____ to know how it goes on.

07 She was a/an _____ gardener, who displayed a creative impulse in gardening.

08 Mr. Hutchison has _____ that he might not be able to continue.

09 A fly buzzing around in my room almost drove me _____ last night.

10 This is a/an _____ book, giving me much useful information on the universe.

LESSON TWENTY-SIX

Target Words

1. Jaded
2. Judgmental
3. Laudatory
4. Light-hearted
5. Ludicrous
6. Irreverent
7. Malicious
8. Mean-spirited
9. Melancholy
10. Mock

LESSON TWENTY-SIX

A. Dictation

____ /10

B. Fill in the blanks with the most appropriate words

01 She was _____ about the whole business of politics, showing no respect for things that were taken seriously.

02 It wasn't a _____ laugh, but it hurt us anyway.

03 The sad _____ drifted through the speakers, and the two of them sat in silence as the song floated through the room.

04 They _____ him because he kept falling off his bike. Soon, he had enough of his friends' _____ laughter.

05 It's definitely not an entertaining, cheery or _____ book at all, but I enjoyed it anyway.

06 I confess to have become so _____ as to find the practice rather boring.

07 Their comments tend to be not just factual but _____, yet they believe they are not making any mistake.

08 The New York Times has this very _____ article about the young inventor.

09 It was _____ to suggest that building a wall along the border can solve the security problem.

10 He complained that he had been receiving _____ telephone calls at midnight.

LESSON TWENTY-SEVEN

Target Words

1. Mournful
2. Mystified
3. Naïve
4. Narcissistic
5. Nostalgic
6. Nonchalant
7. Oblique
8. Oblivious
9. Observant
10. Ominous

LESSON TWENTY-SEVEN

A. Dictation

____ /10

B. Fill in the blanks with the most appropriate words

01 The Crop Circle phenomenon continues to _____ scientists and the public alike.

02 Mary is so _____; she has an excessive interest in her physical appearance.

03 Recently he has dropped _____ hints about the frustrations and pressures of satisfying the club's aspirations.

04 Ms Stevenson's _____ eye took in every detail.

05 There were _____ dark clouds gathering overhead; the slaughter was about to begin.

06 Unbelievably, they can walk among their moaning victims, _____ to their humanity.

07 Only a very _____ observer would conclude that there are only a few threats and dangers to world peace and security today.

08 He looked _____, even near to tears, waving bye bye at the gate.

09 Beneath his apparent _____, he is as nervous and excited as the rest of us.

10 In her art, she said she attempted to evoke the _____ beauty of the good old days.

LESSON TWENTY-EIGHT

Target Words

1. Oppressive
2. Outraged
3. Outspoken
4. Overjoyed
5. Overwhelming
6. Pathetic
7. Patronising
8. Passionate
9. Perplexing
10. Persuasive

LESSON TWENTY-EIGHT

A. Dictation

____ /10

B. Fill in the blanks with the most appropriate words

01 The _____ afternoon heat had quite tired him out.

02 She was _____ to hear that she had got admitted to Harvard University.

03 My auntie was good-hearted and took pity on my _____ form whenever I was sent to the kitchen by my mother.

04 It's her _____ tone that I can't bear; she thought I was too stupid to understand Macbeth.

05 Outside work, Mr. Davidson has always been _____ about sport, especially football and golf.

06 Some leaders have been _____ in their support for political reform in Kenya.

07 Many people were _____ at the bombing, which was nothing but a/an _____.

08 They find the company's attitude _____ and difficult to understand.

09 Your arguments are very _____, but I will not change my mind.

10 Mary is such a gossip that she always feels a/an _____ urge to tell someone about what just happened.

LESSON TWENTY-NINE

Target Words

1. Philosophical
2. Playful
3. Pleading
4. Pragmatic
5. Pretentious
6. Prodigious
7. Provocative
8. Realism
9. Reassured
10. Rebellious

LESSON TWENTY-NINE

A. Dictation

____/10

B. Fill in the blanks with the most appropriate words

01 She is a _____, a truly talented pianist.

02 You will also need to be _____ about what you expect from your family.

03 Her teachers regard her as a _____, trouble-making girl who resists any order that comes her way.

04 Mary is absurdly _____ about the death of her puppy – accepting it as one of God's lessons for her.

05 He was on his knees, and his _____ tone of voice made it impossible for Mary to say no to him.

06 Mike believes, in his book, he deals with grand themes, so whenever he is asked about his book, his response is full of _____ nonsense.

07 My daughter used to play with the kids next door; they were as _____ as kittens.

08 In business, the _____ approach to problem is often more successful than an idealistic one.

09 In a deliberately _____ speech, she criticized the whole system of government.

10 Shelly was so worried about her test result, but her dad's _____ pat on the back removed her fears.

LESSON THIRTY

Target Words

1. Reflective
2. Relieved
3. Reluctant
4. Resentful
5. Resignation
6. Resilient
7. Resourceful
8. Restrained
9. Restless
10. Revolting

LESSON THIRTY

A. Dictation

____ /10

B. Fill in the blanks with the most appropriate words

01 Dan was such a great employee; I accepted his resignation with great _____.

02 She is very _____ to change and her natural _____ always helps her overcome any crisis.

03 I know Mary has to leave me because her dad does not like me. However, she did not even try to change her dad's mind, and her _____ look really upset me.

04 Thomas Edison was amazingly inventive and _____, and he played a major role in the creation of the first industrial research laboratory.

05 We were _____ by the dirt and mess in her house.

06 In the doctor's office, the children grew _____ with the long wait.

07 I was expecting him to be furious, but he was actually very _____, when his girlfriend decided to break up with him.

08 After hearing the news, they sat in a quiet, _____ silence, thinking carefully about what to say.

09 I'm so _____ to find you – I thought you'd already been kidnapped.

10 He harbours a deep _____ towards his parents for his miserable childhood.

LESSON THIRTY-ONE

Target Words

1. Ridiculing
2. Righteous
3. Sarcastic
4. Satirical
5. Scorching
6. Scold
7. Scornful
8. Sceptical
9. Sentimental
10. Sensationalistic

LESSON THIRTY-ONE

A. Dictation

____ /10

B. Fill in the blanks with the most appropriate words

01. The newspaper has been accused of _____ in its coverage of the murders.

02. Many experts remain _____ about his claim that he has found life on Mars.

03. It's true that this movie is bitingly _____, mocking London life in the late 1980s.

04. Even though we are all flawed, we expect public figures to be morally _____.

05. As a heavy child, she became the object of _____ from classmates.

06. I felt like I was walking in an endless desert, with the afternoon sun _____ my skin.

07. In fact, the only laughter he had heard from her was either _____ or sarcastic, and it was usually directed at him.

08. She felt a _____ attachment to the house where she grew up creep over her.

09. If I walk in with muddy boots, Dad always _____ me. If I come home late, Mum will definitely give me a _____ too.

10. "Thanks so much for your help," David said _____, when Jeff broke David's glasses.

LESSON THIRTY-TWO

Target Words

1. Serene
2. Severe
3. Short-tempered
4. Sinister
5. Solemn
6. Sophisticated
7. Stubborn
8. Submissive
9. Superficial
10. Sympathetic

LESSON THIRTY-TWO

A. Dictation

____ /10

B. Fill in the blanks with the most appropriate words

01. There are _____ penalties for failing to declare all your income to the tax authorities.

02. The ruined house had a _____ appearance, making us feel that something evil might happen in there.

03. He was famed for his _____ resistance and his refusal to accept defeat.

04. The analysis of the issues was actually very _____, since it involves only the most obvious things.

05. I don't have much _____ for her – I think she has brought her troubles on herself.

06. They are very _____ observers of the foreign policy scene, intelligent and able to understand complicated situations.

07. I'm a bit _____ sometimes, especially when people keep trying to distract me.

08. In spite of the panic, she remained _____ and in control. It was hard for me not to admire her _____ in the midst of so much chaos.

09. His expression changed from a cheery smile to a _____ frown.

10. George was looking for a quiet _____ wife who would obey his every word. That's why he was hopelessly single.

LESSON THIRTY-THREE

Target Words

1. Talkative
2. Thoughtful
3. Timid
4. Toll
5. Trapped
6. Unassuming
7. Uncooperative
8. Uneasy
9. Unquestioning
10. Unselfish

LESSON THIRTY-THREE

A. Dictation

____/10

B. Fill in the blanks with the most appropriate words

01 For the last 20 years, I have been a/an _____ supporter of public schools.

02 He was shy and _____, and not at all how you expect a celebrity to be.

03 Lucy is as _____ as a rabbit; she has no courage or confidence in herself.

04 When someone just mentioned buying bonds, he suddenly became very _____ , his face slightly flushed, his eyes much bigger.

05 Winter takes its _____ on Jason's health; he now stands an aging man.

06 Tracy became _____: unwilling to do her homework or help with any household chores.

07 Mary started to get a reputation as a/an _____ girl with a heart of gold.

08 Richard was _____ about how best to approach his elderly mother for a loan.

09 George is a bank clerk, who thinks of himself as _____ in the mundane job.

10 Thank you for calling 911 when I was ill – it was very _____ of you.

LESSON THIRTY-FOUR

Target Words

1. Uplifted
2. Upstanding
3. Victorious
4. Vindictive
5. Violent
6. Virtuous
7. Whimsical
8. Witty
9. Wistful
10. Wretched

LESSON THIRTY-FOUR

A. Dictation

____ /10

B. Fill in the blanks with the most appropriate words

01 "If only I had known you then," he said _____, knowing he could never have those days in Spain back.

02 Believe it or not, he only does that charity work so that he can feel _____ with himself.

03 The _____ team were loudly cheered by their fans.

04 Her nationally praised seminars, articles, and books have _____ hundreds of thousands of lives.

05 Jenny has become a _____ woman desperate for revenge against the man who loved and left her.

06 John was known as a _____ man who often changed the colour of his car to fit his mood.

07 His _____ Chevrolet has just broken down again.

08 For the play to be a real success, he himself has made inventive and _____ use of the Glasgow dialect in much of his work.

09 Whenever anything went wrong, he could fly into a _____ rage.

10 These people are modest, _____, hard-working people and a lot of us could learn a lesson or two from them in how to deal with challenges in life.

LESSON THIRTY-FIVE

Target Words

1. Wrangle
2. Wrath
3. Wry
4. Yawn
5. Yawp
6. Yearn
7. Yelp
8. Zeal
9. Zenith
10. Zodiac

LESSON THIRTY-FIVE

A. Dictation

____/10

B. Fill in the blanks with the most appropriate words

01 His unruly behaviour at school incurred the principal's _____.

02 The professor's lecture was so boring that he began _____ and looking at his watch.

03 I suppose it's because I used to live in a crowded city that I am _____ for open spaces in the country.

04 David is a _____ advocate for the rights and freedom of immigrants and others.

05 Venus returns to the same portion of the _____ over a period of exactly eight years.

06 Do you realize that this moment represents the _____ of your success?

07 I accidentally trod on the dog's paw, and it _____.

08 I _____ when you stopped breathing because in you is my own wish to survive.

09 I gave him a _____ smile and commented, "Well done, you have just perfectly ruined my fun."

10 The children were _____ with each other over the new toy.

LESSON ONE

Target Words

1. Abide
2. Ablaze
3. Abolish
4. Acclaimed
5. Accountability
6. Accustom
7. Acknowledge
8. Affection
9. Affectionate
10. Anticipation

A. Fill in the blanks with the most appropriate words.

01 The police officer gave him a ticket because he was not _____ by the law.

02 He had worked very hard on his school project, and the teacher _____ this by giving him a passing grade.

03 The crowd watched the swimmer high up on the diving board, _____ his jump.

04 When you live in a foreign country long enough, you start to feel _____ to their way of life.

05 They drove away from the wildfires, through the forest that had been set _____.

06 She isn't a very _____ person, but that doesn't mean she is unkind.

07 The US _____ slavery in 1865, though it never should have been allowed in the first place!

08 Stephen King has written close to 100 books. He is an _____ horror novelist.

09 If you steal, make no mistake: you will be held _____ for your crime.

10 He had _____ her mistake, and he was prepared to correct it before she had even messed up.

LESSON ONE

B. Fill in the blanks in the passage with the most appropriate words.

Passage 1:

Global warming, or climate change, has become a hotly debated subject among _____ scientists and world politicians alike. In some countries, recycling is required by law, and those who do not _____ by those laws can be fined a lot of money! It has become impossible not to _____ the effect mankind has had on the Earth's environment. Many scientists _____ the atmosphere will continue warming in the coming years unless drastic measures are taken to combat global warming. We must be held _____ for our damage to the Earth because it's coming back around to bite us! Each year, more forests are _____ with wildfires, and in hurricane-prone regions, people have become _____ to worsening storms. One way in which we could reduce pollution is by _____ the production of plastics, which are extremely harmful to the Earth. This is because plastics take thousands of years to deteriorate. We must treat the Earth with love and _____ because it is our home, and we are its caretakers!

LESSON TWO

Target Words

1. Appall
2. Appeal
3. Awkward
4. Barren
5. Belligerent
6. Boundary
7. Brittle
8. Burial
9. Cargo
10. Caution

A. Fill in the blanks with the most appropriate words.

01 The construction workers had just begun repaving the road, so there were many signs telling drivers to exercise _____ and drive slowly.

02 The drought hurt farmers especially. Their fields were _____, and they were unable to harvest many crops that season.

03 She is a vegetarian and finds it _____ that anyone would choose to eat meat.

04 Inmates at the jail can speak to their loved ones, but they find it _____ doing so through glass partitions.

05 He didn't understand the _____ of football. Instead, he found it quite boring.

06 They drank so much alcohol that they became _____, but also tipsy to the point that they could hardly stand up!

07 His father had left a will, which requested that he be _____ rather than cremated.

08 Giant trucks on the highway are usually carrying bulk _____ to different parts of the country.

09 In her old age, she grew weak, and her bones became _____.

10 It is important for professors to establish _____ between themselves and their students. That way, the professors are less likely to play favourites.

LESSON TWO

B. Fill in the blanks in the passage with the most appropriate words.
Passage 2:

The United States and Mexico share an enormously wide border. Recently, right-wing conservatives in the US are calling for a bigger _____ to be placed between the two countries. To many US citizens, the idea of a giant wall separating Mexico and the US is _____. To others, it is _____. Mexico is a big trading partner with the US, and some feel that the addition of such an enormous wall will make transporting _____ like avocados and other goods much more _____. The argument for the wall is not necessarily a _____ one, but such a barrier would put many families in danger of deportation, or of being separated. Admittedly, border patrol can be a difficult and lonely job, no doubt owing to the fact that the patrol area is _____ and devoid of people. Opponents of the wall have _____ supporters, urging them to see that Mexico and the US have a symbiotic relationship, and not at all a _____ or problematic one.

LESSON THREE

Target Words

- Cautious
- Clumsiness
- Clumsy
- Controversial
- Coincidental
- Commodity
- Commonplace
- Complexity
- Conscience
- Contentment

A. Fill in the blanks with the most appropriate words.

01. Because of her constant _____ and poor manners, people were hesitant to invite her to parties.

02. Unfortunately, homelessness is fairly _____ in cities like New York and Los Angeles.

03. She received her paycheck late, so for a few days she could not afford _____ like milk or bread.

04. His raunchy performance at the award show was deemed _____ by tabloids the following day.

05. They are conspiracy theorists, and are always able to find vague _____ in every event they consider suspicious.

06. If she wasn't so _____, she might not have broken the brand new vase.

07. Black holes are a fascinating cosmic phenomenon, but their sheer _____ is enough to turn many people away from studying them.

08. His guilty _____ was enough to drive him mad, so he turned himself in to the police.

09. Yoga is a meditative source of _____ for many people.

10. The ground was uneven, so they had to be _____ of where they stepped.

LESSON THREE

B. Fill in the blanks in the passage with the most appropriate words.
Passage 3:

Social media has become a prevalent part of society. It is even _____ now for children to have social media accounts like Facebook or Instagram. But the topic of social media gives rise to _____ debates. How young is too young for someone to share their lives on social media? Parents should be especially _____ with how they allow their children to interact with people online, and make sure their children practice online safety, if only to clear their own _____! Even the most innocent _____ online can have disastrous consequences.

The _____ of the issue stems from the tendency for many social media users to share too much information, including their whereabouts and goings-on of their daily lives. It is no _____ then that social media has become a unique and dangerous outlet for crime. Some criminals have even been so shortsighted as to share their illegal activity online. These _____ mistakes will often cost them time in prison and make acquiring a job in the future much more difficult. In short, we need to remember that social media is not a _____, but a source of sharing, connecting, and presentation. As long as people are _____, there is still much _____ to be found in meeting new online friends and staying in touch with old ones through social media.

LESSON FOUR

Target Words

1. Context
2. Cynical
3. Deceit
4. Decoration
5. Defy
6. Denial
7. Denote
8. Dependent
9. Deter
10. Determination

A. Fill in the blanks with the most appropriate words.

01. Though he lacked the qualifications necessary for the job, his inadequacies did not _____ him from turning in an application.

02. The burglar stood on trial for his crimes but his _____ of them only made the jury angry; ultimately, he was charged with theft and sentenced to two years in jail.

03. The pathologist studied the cells under a microscope and saw the mutated gene, which indeed _____ the disease the subject was suspected of carrying.

04. The president said something that, when taken out of _____, completely changed the meaning of what he was trying to convey.

05. His _____ and willpower would ensure he received a passing grade.

06. Everyone was under the impression that she would not win the election, but in the end, she _____ all expectation.

07. Craft stores are the best place to buy art supplies and _____ for every kind of event!

08. Her roommate had stolen her wallet, and this _____ was not something she would easily forget.

09. James and Donna are completely _____ upon one another. They are never apart and have to do everything together.

10. She is not very trusting of strangers, and therefore _____ of everyone's motives.

# LESSON FOUR

B. Fill in the blanks in the passage with the most appropriate words.
Passage 4:

The Olympics are an international sporting event. It is a gathering of athletes so adept at their respective sports that they often _____ all expectations, and sometimes even the laws of physics! However, there are many measures taken to ensure none of the athletes cheat. Drug tests are administered in part to _____ the use of performance-enhancing drugs like steroids. In the past, steroid-using athletes could perform at the Olympics without their _____ being detected. This is unfair to those athletes who perform solely using their _____ and natural strength. But now, if athletes are proved to have been using steroids, they are _____ the privilege of competing, and are usually subject to harsh criticism from the media and general public. Cheating _____ dishonesty, and the Olympics are supposed to be about fair play.

Though many people may be _____ of a _____ athlete's genuine abilities, they should remember that not all people will stoop so low as to cheat. The majority of athletes have zero _____ on performance-enhancing drugs, and instead they rely completely on their own athletic ability and rigourous training. In the _____ of the Olympics, however, sometimes, skepticism is necessary.

LESSON FIVE

Target Words

1. Discard
2. Distracted
3. Discreet
4. Diverse
5. Down-to-earth
6. Drift
7. Easy-going
8. Egotism
9. Embarrassment
10. Endure

A. Fill in the blanks with the most appropriate words.

01. The victims of the hurricane had experienced many terrible things, but ultimately, they would _____ and recover from the tragedy.

02. She broke off her friendship with Brooke due to her undeniable _____. Every time Lena tried to talk to her, Brooke would turn the subject back around to herself.

03. They fell asleep as the boat that carried them _____ further and further down the calm, quiet river.

04. After getting a new driver's license, he was finally able to _____ his old one.

05. I tried to do my homework, though I couldn't help but feel _____ by the parade outside my window.

06. He had judged her too early: despite being immaculately dressed and having perfect posture, she was surprisingly _____ and fun to be around.

07. On opening night, the lead actor forgot one of his lines, and even the audience could sense his _____ and complete mortification.

08. They were planning a surprise party for their daughter's birthday and had to be very _____ when decorating the house so as not to ruin the surprise!

09. New Orleans is a lively city full of music and _____ groups of people looking to have fun.

10. She hid her anxiety well, because most people described her as _____.

LESSON FIVE

B. Fill in the blanks in the passage with the most appropriate words.
Passage 5:

Each year, big cities' populations grow by the thousands. But these enormous metropolitan areas are not suitable for everyone. For starters, it is easy to feel _____ in big cities. There is so much going on at once. People who choose to move to a big city must realize that being _____ and _____ is practically a necessity, otherwise they are bound to become stressed. If you can _____ the constant buzz of traffic and people, you might find you'll enjoy the big city. There is much _____ to be found in places like New York, London, Seoul, and Tokyo.

Big cities are not great places for _____ people, though. With metropolises, there comes a sense of anonymity. There are so many people around that it's easy to blend in and become a _____ member of society. If you move to a city and find that you dislike it, you shouldn't feel _____. Don't be so quick to _____ the urban lifestyle. Big cities are centres of culture, and there is always something to do. However, you might be more of a _____ and find that you prefer to move around more often, which is also perfectly ok!

LESSON SIX

Target Words

1. Energize
2. Eternity
3. Ethical
4. Exhilaration
5. Faith
6. Flourish
7. Forgery
8. Fragrance
9. Frustration
10. Gentleness

A. Fill in the blanks with the most appropriate words.

01 Many of the small dogs at the shelter were frantic and jumpy, but it was the _____ of the biggest dog that won her affection.

02 After two cups of coffee, she was so _____ that her hands began to shake.

03 _____ of another person's signature on legal documents is punishable by law.

04 Welfare is a hotly disputed _____ debate of which many people have vastly different opinions.

05 Rush hour traffic was bad enough, but his _____ only took a turn for the worse when someone rear-ended his car.

06 The incoming tornado saw people of all kinds of _____ come together at the church to pray for the town and their loved ones.

07 When he married her, he promised to love her for all _____ --"until death do us part."

08 She gave her sister a bottle of perfume for Christmas, but ultimately, she returned it to the store because she thought its _____ was absolutely putrid!

09 Male peacocks _____ their enormous fan of colourful feathers in hopes that it will impress a female peacock looking for a prospective mate.

10 Roller coasters are a source of _____ for a lot of people, but for others it just makes them frightened or sick.

LESSON SIX

B. Fill in the blanks in the passage with the most appropriate words.
Passage 6:

The Art Museum curator never believed the Picasso painting was _____. It had been shipped overseas to his museum, and people from all over the state had come to see it. Picasso's artwork was always _____ and inspiring to look at. The curator could spend an _____ studying Picasso's work alone and never get bored. The paint _____ on each of Picasso's paintings were masterfully smooth, and he had _____ that no artist alive would be able to replicate the skill with which Picasso painted.

One day, a gallery owner from another city came to the museum to see the painting. The curator was _____ to hear that another art enthusiast would be there to discuss Picasso's work. The gallery owner, a tall woman who was well-dressed and wore a sweet _____, saw the painting and instantly claimed it was a _____. The curator tried to dispute this with as much _____ as he could, but her insistence soon _____ him to the point that he asked her to leave!

Still, he couldn't shake the feeling that he might actually be wrong. After all, if the painting were indeed forged, the museum that had it shipped to him would need to know. It was an _____ issue, and it needed solving. The museum curator called around and found an expert on Picasso to come and analyze the painting, and to his relief the analyst told him that the Picasso painting was genuine! The curator felt a smug sense of pride at this. He knew Picasso as well as the analyst, and he had been right all along.

LESSON SEVEN

Target Words

1. Giggle
2. Guile
3. Harsh
4. Harvest
5. Hatred
6. Highlight
7. Hoarse
8. Insight
9. Icicle
10. Idolize

A. Fill in the blanks with the most appropriate words.

01. He was blunt in his interactions and often offended people by accident. Sometimes his words came out _____ than he intended.

02. The singer's throat hurt the next day, and his voice was _____.

03. People need to be careful when standing under _____. There have actually been reports of them breaking off and impaling people!

04. The protesters' _____ for the president grew day by day, until finally the president was forced to address their demands.

05. Being studious, she had annotated the book to the point that every other sentence was _____ or underlined in pen.

06. Though she enjoyed them, horror movies rarely frightened her. When she saw the new horror movie in theatres, she couldn't help but _____ at certain scenes. As a result, the people around her became annoyed.

07. Knowing her medical condition gave him better _____ as to why she looked the way she did.

08. Children and teenagers should be more selective of whom they choose to _____. Oftentimes celebrities do not set a good example.

09. The full moon in September is known as the _____ Moon. This is because many fruits and vegetables ripen that time of year, and farmers are able to collect and sell them.

10. He was taken to jail, but his charisma and _____ got him back out.

LESSON SEVEN

B. Fill in the blanks in the passage with the most appropriate words.
Passage 7:

The Ravenwood farm was one of the town's best places for autumn activities. Each year, the family who owned the farm, the Ravenwoods, would invite people from all over the state to come _____ pumpkins from their pumpkin patch, run around the corn maze, and go on hayrides. Mr. Ravenwood loved the fall and didn't understand some people's _____ for the season. He knew that some people thought the _____ of the year was summer, with all its warmth and sunlight, but he and his family had always _____ the cold, blustery days of September, October, and November. Even the _____ cold days of winter were fine by him! Enormous _____ dripped down from their barn, which was always an incredible sight to see in the winter.

This year, the Ravenwoods had decided to set up a "haunted house" on their farm. They had gotten some _____ into other popular fall attractions in the city, and learned that scary attractions brought in more money and bigger crowds. Mrs. Ravenwood was especially innovative when it came to setting up the haunted house, and her _____ and creativity made it a complete success. By the end of the weekend, everyone in the Ravenwood family was _____ from all the cheering and _____, and exhausted from providing so much wholesome, autumn fun to the people in their town.

LESSON EIGHT

Target Words

1. Immerse
2. Inspiration
3. Intense
4. Isolate
5. Justified
6. Materialistic
7. Merchandise
8. Mischievous
9. Misinterpret
10. Mistrust

A. Fill in the blanks with the most appropriate words.

01. After the shipwreck, he was able to take shelter on a small island in the middle of the ocean. Devoid of company, he felt immensely _____ and lost all hope of being rescued.

02. People call her _____ because she has expensive taste and frequently treats herself to costly shopping sprees.

03. He preferred reading to watching movies. In his opinion, books were more _____ and characterizations more in-depth.

04. After the concert, they went to the _____ stand to buy a t-shirt with the band's name on it.

05. She was right to _____ her grandson because she discovered that he'd stolen money from her purse while she wasn't looking.

06. It's easy to _____ what a person is saying if you don't speak their language very well.

07. Whenever the painter needs _____, he goes to the beach to people-watch.

08. The cop pulled over Evelyn for turning right without signaling. She _____ her actions by saying she wasn't aware it was against the law.

09. The action movie was too _____ for his liking, so he left halfway through.

10. Foxes are known for their _____ nature. In many cultures, they symbolize cunning and wisdom

LESSON EIGHT

B. Fill in the blanks in the passage with the most appropriate words.
Passage 8:

Chester the mall security guard was _____ of the many shoppers who frequented the mall. In particular, there was a group of three _____ teenaged boys who always seemed to be up to no good. Their antics were never-ending, but Chester had never caught them in the act of a crime, so he had never been able to _____ reprimanding them. Despite the mall being full of people, Chester often felt _____. His job was not as _____ as he had hoped it would be years back when he had applied. Initially, he had wanted to be a police officer!

One day while Chester was on his work break, he was reading a crime novel. He liked crime novels because the heroes who caught the bad guys were a big source of _____ for him. Crime novels were always _____ and exciting! Suddenly Chester saw the three troublemaking boys running down a hallway, their arms full of sports _____. The store manager was yelling at the thieves to stop, crying out for help. This was impossible to _____: the boys had stolen something! He ran after the boys and eventually tackled all of them to the ground. Chester put handcuffs on them, and the sports merchandise was returned to the store manager. The young thieves' _____ antics had at last cost them their freedom, if only for the day.

LESSON NINE

Target Words

1. Numb
2. Nuisance
3. Obscene
4. Observe
5. Optimism
6. Outcome
7. Outdated
8. Outlook
9. Palatable
10. Pale

A. Fill in the blanks with the most appropriate words.

01. The movie was given an R rating for its _____ and excessive displays of violence.

02. Her weakened immune system had not been able to combat the flu. While her face became more and more _____, other more serious symptoms set in

03. The man's leg was _____ using anesthetics so the doctors could extract the bullet lodged in his calf muscle without his feeling unbearable pain.

04. The president had massively understated the dire situation the country was now facing by calling the event a mere _____ on live TV. After that, people began to call for his impeachment.

05. Unfortunately, many countries still exercise _____, discriminatory laws when it comes to gay marriage.

06. Kevin threw a dinner party for his close friends despite his inability to cook very well. The food he prepared for his guests was _____, but by no means delicious.

07. Therapy had helped him appreciate the importance of gratefulness. As a result, his _____ on life had become more positive.

08. National Geographic photographers are very careful when _____ animals in their natural habitat. They do not want to disturb them in any way.

09. He placed a bet on the football team, fully confident they would win the game, but his _____ waned as the opposing team scored over and over again.

10. Campaigns are important, but ultimately, it's electoral votes that determine the _____ of the American presidential race.

LESSON NINE

B. Fill in the blanks in the passage with the most appropriate words.
Passage 9:

Nora hadn't taken her ten-year-old son Richie out to see a movie for a long time. She didn't like going to the theatre because there were too many _____. People talked during the movie, the floor was sticky from spilled sodas, and sometimes it was hard to find a good seat. The _____ of all of this was that she never went to movies, so neither did her son. She decided movie theatres were becoming _____ anyway; with all of the different movie-streaming websites, it was increasingly easier to watch films from the comfort of one's home.

But Richie was desperate to see a new action movie. He begged and begged, and finally Nora gave in. In fact, she even felt _____ about going to see the movie because she had _____ the movie's many great reviews in the newspaper that morning. When they got to the theatre, it was packed and noisy, which instantly dampened her _____ on the experience. She had bought candy for Richie, but none for herself. To her, candy was not _____, which was something Richie would never understand.

Soon the movie started, and within the first thirty minutes, Nora regretted taking her son to see it. It was _____! There was far too much violence and bad language. She didn't like to watch violent things, and soon she felt nauseous. Her face went _____, and she dragged her son out of the theatre. Richie was upset; he had actually been enjoying the movie! Nora later realized Richie hadn't been affected by the violence as much as she had because of all the gruesome video games he regularly played!

LESSON TEN

Target Words

1. Pessimism
2. Practicality
3. Predominant
4. Prejudice
5. Prematurely
6. Preserve
7. Progressive
8. Prospect
9. Recognize
10. Recollect

A. Fill in the blanks with the most appropriate words.

01. _____ is a plague on society. Such misguided hatred often results in violence.

02. In order to _____ uncovered artifacts, archaeologists have to be careful when excavating historical sites.

03. He had been in a car crash recently, so the _____ of getting into a car again was not very likely.

04. His _____ caused many of his friends to stop talking to him.

05. The song started _____ and revealed that the singer was only lip-syncing, which caused a big controversy.

06. Vancouver is a fairly _____ city in regard to the environment.

07. Calico cats are a _____ female breed. This is because the calico gene is linked to the X-chromosome.

08. Dustin immediately _____ his brother's car as soon as it drove up to the airport terminal.

09. Alzheimer's disease inhibits a person's ability to _____ parts of their past.

10. Though the _____ of the prank is debatable, he will go through with it anyway.

100

 # LESSON TEN

B. Fill in the blanks in the passage with the most appropriate words.
Passage 10:

_____ is an unfortunate aspect of society that has become more prevalent and problematic with time. In countries with one _____ ethnicity, minority groups can often feel ostracized. But _____ judging a person based on their race or ethnicity is an unfair thing to do. Too often people are mistrustful of certain groups of people, and this _____ can sometimes lead to violence. The _____ of racism and prejudice are unfounded and can do no good.

Wishing to appear more _____, some cities in the Southern United States have begun to tear down Confederate statues accused of _____ racist cultural beliefs. People are being encouraged to _____ statues of well-known Confederate generals like Robert E. Lee or Nathan Bedford Forrest as symbols of violence, hatred, and prejudice rather than peace, love, and community. _____ and memorializing their triumphs is believed to do more harm than good. The _____ of a world without prejudice is a beautiful one, but it will take a lot of work to get there.

LESSON ELEVEN

Target Words

1. Reckless
2. Reel
3. Reflection
4. Refurbish
5. Relive
6. Reluctant
7. Respected
8. Respectful
9. Reverence
10. Rewarding

A. Fill in the blanks with the most appropriate words.

01 One of the reasons people take videos at concerts is so that later they can _____ the experience.

02 Women should be _____ and cover their hair when visiting a mosque, even if she is not Muslim.

03 A black circle in the top right corner of a movie frame indicates to the projectionist that he/she needs to ready the next _____ of film.

04 Driving without a seatbelt is _____, not to mention very dangerous!

05 The painting conveyed a foreboding _____ on society's addiction to technology.

06 _____ animals when they have properly obeyed a command is an essential part of training.

07 He _____ her writing style despite the fact that he found the story itself to be dull and unoriginal.

08 They had gotten food poisoning from the restaurant down the street, so they were _____ _____ to eat there ever again.

09 Military funerals are always emotional displays of _____ for fallen soldiers.

10 He bought the apartment on a whim, but it was only after close inspection that he realized how badly the place needed _____.

LESSON ELEVEN

B. Fill in the blanks in the passage with the most appropriate words.
Passage 11:

Dale and Diane bought a house together. They knew it would need _____, but they were determined to make a home for themselves. Initially they had been _____ to buy a house because of how much upkeep ownership can require. Still, they were not _____ people and knew they could take care of the house as long as they were _____ of the place and took good care of it. Besides, owning a house for the first time seemed like a very _____ experience, and they were ready to start a family.

They found the house through an ad in a home magazine. Beneath the ad was the phone number for a very _____ local realtor. They called the realtor and set up an appointment to see the house. When Dale and Diane got to the house, they stood in _____ of its simplistic beauty. It was a two-storey white brick house with green shutters, and it was perfect! They instantly knew it was the house for them. After a bit of _____ on their financial status, they told the realtor they wanted to buy it. The realtor was _____; she was so relieved someone had finally bought it! It had been on the market for some time, but at last it had found its owners. Dale and Diane signed the papers and later that night they drank celebratory glasses of champagne while discussing their plans for the house. It was a happy day they would always be able to _____ and look back on with a smile.

LESSON TWELVE

Target Words

1. Ritual
2. Rub
3. Run-down
4. Rustle
5. Scent
6. Scrap
7. Selfish
8. Self-sufficient
9. Shabby
10. Shatter

A. Fill in the blanks with the most appropriate words.

01. He has been _____ since he was sixteen years old, and is never without a well-paying job.

02. Stonehenge, a prehistoric landmark in England, is believed to be a place where pagan _____ were once performed.

03. After hearing gunshots outside her house one night, Annie resolved to move out of the _____ neighbourhood and into a safer one.

04. In October, it seems as if the _____ of pumpkin is always in the air, wherever you go.

05. The slums of Rio de Janeiro are packed with _____ houses inhabited by people of low-income, as well as the unemployed.

06. The man at the bar would not stop staring at her, and she was beginning to feel uncomfortable. Something about his unwavering gaze _____ her the wrong way.

07. They were told he was quite the gentleman, but by showing up drunk to their house, he _____ all of their expectations.

08. She ran through the forest, the _____ of leaves around her providing a peaceful soundtrack to her workout.

09. It was _____ of him to take the last two slices of pizza, especially considering he didn't help pay for it.

10. The junkyard is full of _____ metal. Oftentimes, the more valuable kinds are looted.

LESSON TWELVE

B. Fill in the blanks in the passage with the most appropriate words.
Passage 12:

After graduating high school, Alana decided she didn't want to go to college. However, she wanted to be _____ and financially independent from her parents, so she moved out. Alana moved into a _____ apartment in a _____ part of town; sadly, it was all she could afford at the time.

The first night in her apartment, she could barely sleep. It was cold, and her apartment didn't have very good heating, so she piled on sweaters and _____ her arms to keep warm. The trees outside tapped on her bedroom window, their leaves _____ in the wind. She lit a lavender-_____ candle to put her nerves at ease, a nighttime _____ she had adopted years ago, and tried to relax.

She wondered if her parents thought she was _____ for moving out, but they had been understanding. Without her living at home, her parents could _____ her from their list of monthly expenses—she was one less mouth to feed! They knew Alana had never been interested in going to college, so she was relieved to find that she hadn't _____ any of their expectations. She was content with a simple education and a simple job.

LESSON THIRTEEN

Target Words

1. Solitude
2. Spite
3. Split
4. Spontaneity
5. Stiff
6. Still
7. Strict
8. Suspenseful
9. Thrill
10. Timeless

A. Fill in the blanks with the most appropriate words.

01. He left a terrible scratch on the side of her car, so out of _____ she did the same to his.

02. Crime shows are my favourite because of the mystery and _____.

03. Her wardrobe is minimalistic. Many of her clothes are classic, _____ garments that will never go out of style.

04. He is the kind of person who favours _____ over predictability.

05. He wasn't sure which way to turn, so at the last second he steered left. This _____ decision cost him a flat tire, because the road to the left was covered in nails.

06. Though it's cheaper to live with roommates, he chooses to live alone. The _____ allows him to do whatever he wants without anyone around to judge him.

07. Once you know the plot twist at the end of the movie, it loses its _____.

08. The _____ of the forest at night was eerie to the campers.

09. We have _____ rules about what constitutes appropriate work-wear.

10. She had gone on a very long run the day before and had not stretched afterwards, so the following day her joints felt very _____.

LESSON THIRTEEN

B. Fill in the blanks in the passage with the most appropriate words.
Passage 13:

She had finally finished reading the horror novel, and boy had it been _____! The story was a _____ tale of murder and intrigue, in which a killer and detective played cat-and-mouse. She liked to read scary stories at night and in complete _____, when everything was quiet and _____, though _____ speaking she didn't confine her reading solely to the evening hours. She had picked the book up on a whim; her _____ in choosing books was habitual, and it was rare for her to re-read anything. She liked reading new books and learning about different authors that she had never before heard of.

She had gotten sick of reading _____ classic novels like To Kill a Mocking Bird and Moby Dick, so partly out of _____ for whar she felt was the pretentious world of literature, she delved into horror and crime novels. Horror and crime books were usually scorned in the literary world, criticized for having weak plotlines and _____ narration. She detested this attitude towards reading. Any reading was better than none, no matter how badly reviewed it might be, or how unpopular it was among academics! Though she had been _____ over which genre to choose, the scary book she had just finished reading had actually ended up being a very interesting one!

LESSON FOURTEEN

Target Words

1. Tolerance
2. Trivia
3. Trot
4. Triumph
5. Uninviting
6. Unique
7. Unmanageable
8. Upbringing
9. Ubiquitous
10. Ultimate

A. Fill in the blanks with the most appropriate words.

01. Reality shows were not her favourite, but she did have a soft spot for _____ shows like Jeopardy.

02. The horses moved along at a steady _____ while the carriage behind bumped and rocked every time the wheels went over a pebble.

03. He hated his birthmark, but his mother told him it made him _____.

04. On her trip abroad she got to see many incredible landmarks, but the _____ sight had been the Eiffel Tower in Paris.

05. From a very young age, she and her siblings had been forced to work on the farm. Needless to say, she didn't have a very pleasant _____.

06. The trick-or-treaters went from one house to the next ringing doorbells, but they all avoided the house on Neibolt Street. The house looked, to say the least, quite _____.

07. Though they had lost the soccer game that day, they knew that they could _____ if they practiced harder.

08. The school has a zero-_____ policy when it comes to plagiarism.

09. She put her hair up because it was being _____. The humidity had made it extremely frizzy.

10. The famous horror novelist Stephen King has had a _____ influence on both horror movies and books.

LESSON FOURTEEN

B. Fill in the blanks in the passage with the most appropriate words.
Passage 14:

The jockey had been training for months. The _____ race was ahead of him, and he had just one more week before he was to compete. The jockey had been raised in a regimented household. His _____ had been an athletic one, and from a young age he knew he wanted to be a jockey. Jockeys are _____ among athletes because their sport favours a smaller stature which he had. Other sports like basketball and football, which were dominated by tall and musclebound men, were far more _____ to him and his body type. In the world of popular sports, the typical male physique was _____ accepted as being very tall and muscular, neither of which the average jockey could claim to be.

The jockey had _____ in horse racing, however. He was able to get along with even the most _____ horses, including the temperamental ones who would buck off their riders despite only moving at a _____ rather than a strenuous gallop. Early on, the universal _____ and respect all horses seemed to have for him had been a sign that this was the sport he should pursue. His insecurities about being small seemed to simply be insignificant _____. He had figured out exactly where, athletically, he fit in best.

LESSON FIFTEEN

Target Words

1. Accepting
2. Accommodating
3. Admiring
4. Adoring
5. Affluent
6. Ambitious
7. Ambivalent
8. Amused
9. Antagonistic
10. Apathetic

A. Fill in the blanks with the most appropriate words.

01. The hotel staff was very _____ towards the family whose luggage was lost on the flight.

02. She is an _____ young woman with dreams of becoming a famous photographer.

03. It was a hot day, so the children tried to fry an egg on the sidewalk. Their mother was not _____.

04. The Red Cross Relief Fund helps those who have been impacted by natural disasters. However, people who are far removed from those tragic events are often _____ to the cause.

05. Lucas absolutely _____ the dog he had seen at the animal shelter, so he adopted him.

06. We try to be _____ of other people, regardless of their ethnicity.

07. She is self-centred and can sometimes be found _____ her own reflection in the mirror.

08. Using an _____ approach during an argument is a sure way to make the other person angry.

09. The television show had mixed reviews. Many people loved it, many hated it, and others were entirely _____.

10. They live in a mansion in an _____ part of town reserved for those with lots of money.

LESSON FIFTEEN

B. Fill in the blanks in the passage with the most appropriate words.
Passage 15:

Restaurant managers have to be extremely good at dealing with people. _____ customers is one of the biggest aspects of their job. They should be _____ of the fact that things will go wrong, customers will sometimes be unhappy, and accidents will happen. Being _____ to the goings-on in their restaurant is simply not an option. Likewise, they must be exceptional decision-makers, as there is little to no room for _____. If they can maintain an air of authority, be an efficient, hard worker, and keep things light and _____, their employees are sure to be respectful and _____. After all, the last thing a manager wants is an _____ environment where people are argumentative and nothing gets done.

In more _____ restaurants, managers can earn greater incomes. But fancy restaurants are not for everyone, and those who work there must be _____ and even more hardworking, as there is very little room for error. But regardless of a restaurant's prestige, we should be _____ of those who work in the food service industry. Those jobs are extremely labour-intensive, the hours are long and tiring, and their primary goal is to make customers happy. So be kind to them— you will both have a better time for it!

LESSON SIXTEEN

Target Words

1. Apologetic
2. Apprehensive
3. Appreciative
4. Argumentative
5. Arrogant
6. Assertive
7. Athletic
8. Benevolent
9. Bewildered
10. Bitter

A. Fill in the blanks with the most appropriate words.

01 Being afraid of heights, he was _____ about diving into the pool from the high board.

02 He is the kind of person who will never admit to any wrongdoings. In short, he is _____.

03 The local gym was packed with _____ types, but she was encouraged when she saw a few overweight people like herself.

04 Raw, unsweetened chocolate is _____. It completely loses its appeal!

05 Though he was _____ about hitting her mailbox with his car, she was nevertheless angry it had happened in the first place.

06 They discussed politics over dinner, and Austin became shockingly _____.

07 Being _____ and straightforward with someone you want to date is a better way to approach the situation than simply keeping quiet.

08 The end of the book _____ her. She was not expecting the main character to die!

09 He was _____ of the shirt his father had given him for his birthday, despite not really liking it very much.

10 The kindergarten teacher was a kind, _____ woman who regarded her students as lovingly as her own children.

Copyright © Icon English All Rights Reserved

112

LESSON SIXTEEN

B. Fill in the blanks in the passage with the most appropriate words.
Passage 16:

The PE coach told the class they would be playing dodgeball, and all of the kids groaned. Most of them thought dodgeball was a mean sport, so many of them were _____ about playing. The _____ kids were excited, though. Some of them were _____ enough to heckle the smaller kids in the class. One of the kids, Lucas, was _____ that the coach was going to make them play dodgeball in the first place. It shouldn't have been much of a surprise to Lucas, though. The coach was not known for his _____. In other classes, the coach sometimes became _____ and tyrannical with children who weren't quite as able-bodied as other students. Lucas assumed the coach was just a/an _____ old man.

The kids who didn't want to play dodgeball had congregated by the edge of the basketball court. Lucas joined them. The kids discussed how they wanted to go complain to the principal, but Lucas _____ told them that that particular strategy wasn't likely to work. He decided the best approach was to be _____ and confront the PE teacher right away. No one else was brave enough, so Lucas volunteered, for which the other kids were very _____. In the end, Lucas's plea for the coach to choose another game was futile. The PE coach just didn't care about their concerns. But luckily for the kids, he was fired one week later!

LESSON SEVENTEEN

Target Words

1. Bold
2. Captivating
3. Callous
4. Candid
5. Caustic
6. Cautionary
7. Celebratory
8. Chaotic
9. Charitable
10. Cheerful

A. Fill in the blanks with the most appropriate words.

01 The photographer prefers to take _____ pictures of people, rather than have them posed and aware of him taking their photo.

02 Hansel and Gretel is a _____ tale that warns children against going into the woods alone and entering the house of a stranger.

03 He is a _____ man. Twice a year he donates clothing to homeless shelters.

04 Asking her on a date was a _____ move, but he was confident she would say yes.

05 Critics called the play _____ and visionary.

06 Weddings are _____ affairs that honour the union of two people in love.

07 A fire broke out in the movie theatre and it soon became _____ as people tried to escape.

08 She is not a very _____ person. She rarely smiles and wears lots of black clothing.

09 I was surprised by how _____ he seemed when discussing the brutal attack shown on the news.

10 Be careful using certain drain cleaners. They can be quite _____, and some might ruin your pipes!

LESSON SEVENTEEN

B. Fill in the blanks in the passage with the most appropriate words.
Passage 17:

The dramatic play had been a _____ story about two _____ friends camping together in an isolated part of the woods. It had begun in a _____ manner, with many comedic moments. Everyone laughed when the actors finally set up the tent, which they had been attempting to do for at least ten minutes, and then again when the actors each gave a _____ holler. The play was so well acted that the audience felt as if they were looking in on a _____, real-life camping trip.

However, the play took a dark turn and soon became a _____ tale of the consequences of being too isolated. The two people started making _____, backhanded comments to one another, and they grew more and more _____ about the other's well-being. They were less _____ to one another than they had been at the start, and soon turned suspicious about the other's intentions. The play reached its _____ climax when one of the friends killed the other, and the survivor escaped the woods to return to civilization. It was a brilliant play, though quite bleak and depressing.

LESSON EIGHTEEN

Target Words

1. Compassionate
2. Complacent
3. Compliant
4. Complimentary
5. Conceited
6. Congenial
7. Condescending
8. Contemptuous
9. Contented
10. Conventional

A. Fill in the blanks with the most appropriate words.

01. He likes to patronize people by speaking to them in _____ ways.

02. The more _____ approach to job-hunting is to speak with an employer directly. But these days, most employers simply require an online application be filled out.

03. His _____ attitude towards the fantasy book series was astounding, especially considering how cherished it was among the masses.

04. It had begun to rain outside, so she curled up on the couch with a book and a cup of tea, feeling warm and _____.

05. Teachers tend to dislike students who are not _____ with their classroom rules.

06. I am amazed at the sheer scope of her _____. She seems to spend half her life in front of a mirror.

07. Mother Teresa is a symbol not only of peace and wisdom, but of _____ as well.

08. The opposing team was so _____ when it came to their winning streak that even their fans grew annoyed with their atttitude.

09. She was glad to leave the hot, humid state of Florida and return to Vancouver, a city with a more _____, moderate climate.

10. It was the boy's birthday, so the restaurant manager offered him a _____ bowl of ice cream.

LESSON EIGHTEEN

B. Fill in the blanks in the passage with the most appropriate words.
Passage 18:

Steve used to be a _____ man who appeared proud and reveled in being _____ to people for no other reason than to upset them. He was _____ too, and treated others as his inferiors. Upsetting people actually _____ him, and he regularly went out of his way to be unkind. Consequently, he didn't have many friends. Few people were _____ enough to be around him for more than a few minutes. It was only after his boss fired him that he began to reconsider his lack of _____. For so long, he had been _____ about being known as a mean person. The infamy was even something he took pride in! But upon losing his job, he wondered if being a more _____ person might make him happier.

For these reasons, he decided to take yoga classes. He wasn't the most _____ type of person to be doing yoga: he was overweight, impatient, and had zero flexibility. But as he progressed in his practice, his yoga teacher became more _____ about his growth and transformation. Steve soon found that he no longer felt the need to shout at people or speak to them in patronizing ways. He was becoming a kind, good-natured person, and within a few months he even had friends and a great new job!

LESSON NINETEEN

Target Words

Courageous	Despairing
Crooked	Detached
Crucial	Dignified
Demeaning	Diplomatic
Depressing	Disapproving

A. Fill in the blanks with the most appropriate words.

01 It was only after putting all of the tiles down that the stonemason realized one of them was _____ and would need to be adjusted.

02 He tried not to feel _____ over the loss of his pet goldfish, but he had owned the creature for over seven years and had grown quite fond of him.

03 During the Cold War, _____ relations between the USA and Soviet Union were extremely tense.

04 Perhaps it was his tall stature or his pristine style of dress, but he had an undeniably _____ look to him.

05 The teacher had been unnecessarily _____ towards the student who had answered the question incorrectly.

06 A _____ ingredient in many Mexican recipes is chilis. Without them, the dish can taste very bland.

07 Jumping off the rocks into the lake below was _____, but also perilous.

08 The movie had a sad ending, and it made her feel _____, so afterwards she bought a new candle to cheer herself up.

09 The character in the book is somewhat _____ from reality. He doesn't seem to understand his actions have consequences!

10 Being very conservative, the father was _____ of his daughter's prom dress, which he considered indecent for a girl her age.

LESSON NINETEEN

B. Fill in the blanks in the passage with the most appropriate words.
Passage 19:

The advisers told the senator that he should participate in a fundraiser to boost his popularity ratings. The senator thought of the motive _____; participating in a fundraiser merely to gain popularity was a bit _____, but he agreed to do it nonetheless. The fundraiser was to be a marathon, but the senator was not much of a runner. _____ about the forthcoming race, his advisers took a _____ approach to the situation and set him up with a physical trainer.

The trainer made him do exercises that he found silly and a bit _____, but the trainer insisted that practice was _____ if he wanted to do well during the marathon. The senator's progress was slow, which he found _____, but after a few weeks he became more physically fit. It wasn't long until he even felt _____ about the marathon, confident that he would do better than he had ever expected. The training had not only made him healthier, but also more _____. He realized too that he was looking forward to the race, not just so that he could run it and impress people, but also because the fundraiser was for a really good cause. Being _____ from his community was not something he could afford with the coming election, and the marathon fundraiser would be beneficial in multiple ways.

LESSON TWENTY

Target Words

1. Disenfranchised
2. Disparaging
3. Distressing
4. Disdained
5. Distraught
6. Disheartened
7. Defeatist
8. Desolate
9. Depressive
10. Determined

A. Fill in the blanks with the most appropriate words.

01 The _____ subject matter of the documentary caused many people to avoid watching it.

02 The new law passed by the president would _____ many immigrants from accessing health care benefits.

03 She had not won the competition, and watched with _____ as the winner collected the trophy.

04 They couldn't help but feel _____ upon receiving the news that the house they had bought only a month ago would in fact need serious renovating due to leaky pipes.

05 She used to be an optimistic person, but after so much bad luck over the past year, she has now become a bit of a _____.

06 I am _____ to make you see the error of your ways!

07 Saving a child from drowning on her first day of work was a _____ way for the lifeguard to start her new job.

08 They drove through the desert, which was _____ and seemingly devoid of life.

09 He was a good lawyer, but sometimes he could be too _____ towards competing law firms.

10 The family's dog had run away, and everyone was _____ until, finally, the dog returned home one morning.

LESSON TWENTY

B. Fill in the blanks in the passage with the most appropriate words.
Passage 20:

Will had decided to participate in the high school talent show that year. Despite his _____ feelings about performing in front of large groups of people, he was _____ to try out. On the day of the tryouts, he went into the school auditorium and was somewhat _____ to see that there were at least one hundred other students there. The _____ in him told him that he should just leave without giving it a shot, but eventually he was able to shut out such _____ thoughts.

He took a seat and watched other students' auditions while he waited. He felt a bit of _____ when he saw how many of them were truly talented, for he thought he might not do quite as well as they. But this _____ line of thinking would only make him more nervous, so he put on a smile and clapped for each young performer. Three teachers at the school would serve as judges for the talent show. In earlier years, students voted during the talent show by round of applause. Eventually, students felt _____ because this method of voting seemed inaccurate.

Soon the auditorium became _____ as more and more students left the tryouts. Eventually it was Will's turn to perform. He had written a song specifically for the talent show. Though he was worried the song might be too mournful and _____, the teacher judges ended up applauding him! Will had at last conquered his stage fright. Now all he had to do was go on to perform at the actual show next week.

LESSON TWENTY-ONE

Target Words

1. Docile
2. Earnest
3. Elated
4. Embarrassed
5. Empathetic
6. Empower
7. Empirical
8. Enchant
9. Engaged
10. Enraged

A. Fill in the blanks with the most appropriate words.

01. Standing in a superhero pose is said to be _____.

02. She could not shake the _____ she felt after tripping and falling down in front of the boy she liked earlier that day.

03. Deer are beautiful, _____ animals that are full of grace.

04. The employee had worked with the company for over forty years, so on his retirement day he was _____ to finally have time to travel and pursue various hobbies

05. Her voice was so _____ that everyone stopped what they were doing and listened to her song.

06. The therapist suggested anger management classes because his patient was easily _____.

07. The professor knew her student would go far in life because of how hardworking and _____ the student was in class.

08. _____ is an important quality for counselors to have.

09. There is plenty of _____ evidence to prove global warming is no hoax.

10. Teddy and Dolores had been dating five years before getting _____.

LESSON TWENTY-ONE

B. Fill in the blanks in the passage with the most appropriate words.
Passage 21:

Abigail had never considered herself a _____ person, but one day she realized she had become a bit too stuck in her ways. Therefore, she decided to do something different and exciting. She had, in _____, always wanted to try skydiving. It seemed like an _____ experience, and her recently _____ cousin had gone skydiving with her fiancé the month before. This cousin had been _____ to tell Abigail about the experience at first. This was because Abigail's cousin had nearly fainted from fear as they boarded the plane. But her cousin's fiancé had convinced her to follow through with the skydiving, and in the end Abigail's cousin had been _____ by how incredible the experience had been.

It was her cousin's positive experience that made Abigail decide to try it out for herself. She was _____ towards her cousin's fear of heights, but _____ evidence proved that facing one's fears often eliminated those anxieties. Abigail decided not to tell her parents; she knew they would be _____ if they found out their own daughter was doing something so reckless. On the day of her skydiving adventure, somewhat _____ by a delirious haze of anticipation, Abigail boarded the skydiving plane with the instructor, and they took off into the sky.

LESSON TWENTY-TWO

Target Words

1. Enthusiasm
2. Entreating
3. Envious
4. Euphoric
5. Evasive
6. Exasperate
7. Fascinate
8. Fatalistic
9. Fearsome
10. Feasible

A. Fill in the blanks with the most appropriate words.

01 Being a bit overweight, he couldn't help but feel _____ when he saw people who were in great shape.

02 Dangerous activities like skydiving and hang-gliding are _____ ways for adrenaline junkies to get their fill of adventure.

03 After a harsh scolding by his boss for being late to work, he only became more _____ when he discovered his car had been towed

04 He was somewhat _____ when it came to seeing his friends. He often cancelled plans at the last minute.

05 I cannot quell my _____ for the movie coming out this Friday. I've been looking forward to seeing it for over a year!

06 Childbirth is a/an _____ experience for fathers, and a painful one for mothers.

07 They had decorated their house with a _____ display for Halloween, complete with ghosts, zombies, and fake spider webs.

08 When it comes to the cosmos, it will take more to _____ an astronomer than a few commonly known facts about black holes.

09 The climber was determined to scale Mount Everest, but his friends and family _____ him to reconsider the dangerous venture.

10 Going to New Zealand is definitely _____, but make no mistake: it will be an expensive trip!

LESSON TWENTY-TWO

B. Fill in the blanks in the passage with the most appropriate words.
Passage 22:

Governments all across the world need to begin _____ their citizens to recycle and take better care of the Earth. Perhaps if such environmentally conscious deeds such as recycling and using public transportation were incentivized, _____ for such things might grow. Take for example the country of Finland. Their miniscule impact on the earth's environment is _____, to say the least. This is because of the strict yet _____ laws its government has enacted to protect the environment. We should all feel some _____ at the fact that not all countries hold themselves to the same standard of environmentally friendly living that Finland has set for its citizens. Being _____ about caring for the environment is, at this point, no longer an option.

It is _____ to consider the possibility that the damage humans have done to the earth might be irreversible. To study the harmful effects mankind has had on our global environment would make a _____ of anyone. Indeed, it would be _____ and _____ to see every country on this planet come together and work towards repairing the world's environment. Species are dying out, Arctic ice caps are melting at alarming rates, and wildfires are more and more prevalent each year. If we work together to take care of the earth, the earth will repay our efforts and slowly begin to heal itself.

LESSON TWENTY-THREE

Target Words

1. Finicky
2. Forceful
3. Frank
4. Frivolous
5. Grateful
6. Grim
7. Gullible
8. High-spirited
9. Hostile
10. Humble

A. Fill in the blanks with the most appropriate words.

01 The doorknob can be _____, so just shake the key inside the lock a few times, and then it will open.

02 Everyone's favourite character in the TV show is known for his courage and _____.

03 I find it best to be as _____ and straightforward with people as possible.

04 Being _____ in an argument is a surefire way to make the other person angry.

05 It was an extremely hot day, and everyone became _____ when the clouds rolled in and the temperatures dropped.

06 The sitcom was inane and _____. It had no intellectual value.

07 Sleepy Hollow is a _____ tale of a murderous headless horseman and the young man recruited to stop him.

08 Mother bears become extremely _____ if their cubs are threatened.

09 The annual Autumn festival is a _____ event where vendors set up shops to sell decorative trinkets, and people from all over the city come to see their wares.

10 The little girl hated to be called _____, though there was some truth to it: just last week her brother had told her the moon was made of cheese, and she had actually believed him!

LESSON TWENTY-THREE

B. Fill in the blanks in the passage with the most appropriate words.
Passage 23:

It was a _____ day at the coffee shop. Outside it was storming, and the _____ rain and wind had kept many potential customers from coming into the café. Don, the manager of the café, was _____ for the gloomy weather, though the two baristas working there that day—Regina and Amy—were not as enthusiastic. There was only one customer in the entire café, so the girls were quite bored. Don tried to be _____ and stay positive, but his _____ approach to the terrible storm outside only seemed to make Regina and Amy _____.

The girls' _____ moods soon irritated him, and he decided that in order to turn their attitudes around, he would make a contest: whoever got the most cleaning done in the next two hours would get to go home early. _____, though, what he thought would end up being a fun game quickly became a disturbing competition, as Amy and Regina both sabotaged the other's work. Don wondered if he had been _____ to assume his contest would lift their spirits. He was only trying to take a sullen afternoon and make it a bit fun by bringing in this _____ activity. By the end of the first hour, though, the storm had begun to subside, and more customers came in. And by the end of the day, the sun was shining again, and Regina and Amy were back to their normal, happy selves! Don just hoped a storm would not roll in again any time soon…

LESSON TWENTY-FOUR

Target Words

1. Humourous
2. Hypercritical
3. Impatient
4. Impartial
5. Implore
6. Incredulous
7. Indecisive
8. Indeterminate
9. Indifferent
10. Indignant

A. Fill in the blanks with the most appropriate words.

01 People running for any political position need to keep in mind that the media will be _____ _____ of their every word.

02 Smoking is terrible for your health. I _____ you to quit!

03 Though she was the lead actress in the film, she was surprisingly _____ when the film won an award.

04 Dogs can be so _____, especially when they chase their own tails!

05 Jurors in high-profile cases must be _____ to both sides upon entering the trial.

06 She grew so _____ with the rush hour traffic that she made an illegal turn in the middle of the road.

07 I grew _____ when they accused me of stealing the phone.

08 The marine biology student was _____ when she learned that the ocean floor has never been fully mapped out.

09 He asked her where she wanted to go for dinner, but her _____ drove him mad. In the end they just stayed at home and cooked a frozen pizza.

10 The age of the artifact is _____, but upon further inspection the scientists will surely be able to discover it.

LESSON TWENTY-FOUR

B. Fill in the blanks in the passage with the most appropriate words.
Passage 24:

Bobby wanted to take his girlfriend, Shelley, out on a date for Valentine's Day, but he was _____ of which restaurant to take her to because he wanted their date to be perfect. He knew that Shelley would be _____ about where they went, just as long as they went somewhere, so her _____ in the matter should have made things easier for Bobby. To the contrary, he was still _____! Within a month, Bobby had visited over ten different restaurants in an attempt to find the most romantic place with the best food and ambiance, but by the end of the month the winning restaurant was still _____.

Bobby was beginning to feel _____. He tried to talk to Shelley about it, and when he told her that he had gone to more than ten different restaurants searching for the perfect place, she laughed! Bobby didn't think it was so _____. In fact, he became somewhat _____ about how nonchalant Shelley was being about the whole thing. Shelley _____ Bobby to quit looking for the perfect place, and told him that anywhere would be fine by her, just as long as they spent Valentine's Day together. _____ though deeply touched, he made a reservation at an Italian restaurant because he knew Shelley loved Italian food, plus the restaurant had gotten great reviews online. And in the end, he knew she was right: it didn't matter where they went, so long as they were together.

LESSON TWENTY-FIVE

Target Words

1. Inexorable
2. Informative
3. Insane
4. Insecure
5. Inspired
6. Intellectual
7. Intimate
8. Intimidate
9. Intangible
10. Intrigued

A. Fill in the blanks with the most appropriate words.

01. The comedy movie was vapid and had no redeeming _____ qualities.

02. Hugging is an _____ show of affection that is usually reserved for close friends and family.

03. The new car's technology was _____. It was somehow able to detect accidents before they happened.

04. _____ asylums are places reserved for those of poor mental health who cannot take care of themselves.

05. An _____ current dragged the canoe closer and closer to the edge of the waterfall.

06. The documentary received a lot of attention, despite the fact that it wasn't very _____.

07. When she was young, she read a book that eventually _____ her to become a writer.

08. Ghosts are said to be _____, phantom-like apparitions.

09. The new president liked _____ other diplomats by using too much force when shaking their hands.

10. After the first Olympic runner ran the one-hundred-meter championship in record-breaking time, the next competitor in line was visibly _____ about following such a historical accomplishment with his own performance.

LESSON TWENTY-FIVE

B. Fill in the blanks in the passage with the most appropriate words.
Passage 25:

Libraries are _____ centres of culture, literature, and community. Books of every subject can be found at most public libraries, ranging from _____ biographies to collections of poetry, from fantasy series to political textbooks, and oftentimes even old newspapers and magazines! Some libraries are massive, while others are small and _____, but each is the same in that they will always retain a great amount of _____ value. A library's importance is never _____, as their most vital resource—books—can be borrowed and held in the palm of your hand!

Books are an everyday part of life, and the thought of a world without books might drive many people to _____. Books can _____ confidence, and reading can even lessen a person's _____ by providing them with the knowledge to change and better themselves. It is lucky that mankind is a species full of curiosity and _____, because libraries will never fall out of relevance. Our _____ need to learn and relate to others is a basic part of humanity, and libraries are temples of wisdom, creativity, and life itself.

LESSON TWENTY-SIX

Target Words

1. Jaded
2. Judgmental
3. Laudatory
4. Light-hearted
5. Ludicrous
6. Irreverent
7. Malicious
8. Mean-spirited
9. Melancholy
10. Mock

A. Fill in the blanks with the most appropriate words.

01 It was not right of him to be so _____ of people with glasses when he himself wore them!

02 He made a _____ joke, but everyone took it too seriously and got offended.

03 The vegetarian dish used _____ chicken, which is actually made of tofu but imitates the taste of chicken.

04 The boy was an _____ student whom many teachers at the school secretly abhorred.

05 There is an undeniable air of _____ about her, despite the fact that she wears bright colours!

06 The prank ended up being far more _____ than they had intended. Afterwards they apologized for letting it get out of hand.

07 She put extra spices into the dish to make sure that even the most _____ of palates would enjoy the meal.

08 The editor's _____ comments on her story made her confident it would soon be published.

09 Though his car had been parked illegally, he found it _____ that they had only waited ten minutes before towing it!

10 He was a _____ man who took pleasure in seeing others hurt.

LESSON TWENTY-SIX

B. Fill in the blanks in the passage with the most appropriate words.
Passage 26:

Daryl, who worked at the bank as an accountant, hadn't always been so _____. He used to be a _____ person who brought joy and laughter whenever he came to work at the bank. In the past, he was quick to offer _____ comments to hardworking employees, and doled out compliments as easily as breathing. But the other bank workers soon wondered if Daryl had become _____ in some way, because his kind comments soon became _____. Whereas he used to be chipper and happy, he was now _____ and sullen. He had even become more _____ of the customers who came into the bank, and once made a mean comment _____ a person for their low bank balance when they were trying to get a loan!

Daryl's boss, Anita, was sick of Daryl's _____ behaviour, and brought him into her office one morning when Daryl's work conduct had been especially _____. She told him that either he could change his attitude or work someplace else. Suddenly, Daryl broke out in tears and told Anita that his wife of ten years had just filed for divorce! None of the bank employees had even noticed that Daryl was no longer wearing his wedding ring. At last Anita understood why Daryl had become so uncharacteristically _____ in such a short while. She told him to take the rest of the week off to recuperate, and by the time he came back Daryl had not only made amends with his wife but was also back to his old, chipper self!

LESSON TWENTY-SEVEN

Target Words

1. Mournful
2. Mystified
3. Naïve
4. Narcissism
5. Nostalgic
6. Nonchalant
7. Oblique
8. Oblivious
9. Observant
10. Ominous

A. Fill in the blanks with the most appropriate words.

01. _____ is a personality disorder that gets its name from a Greek myth about a man who loved himself so much, he drowned trying to embrace his own reflection.

02. People found her to be _____ despite the fact that she had travelled to dozens of countries and had a college degree.

03. He was quiet and _____. Nothing went over his head, and he seemed keenly aware of everything and everyone at all times.

04. The news article contained _____, vindictive remarks about the president that were sure not to go unnoticed by the paper's readers.

05. The television show uses songs from the 80s, which makes him _____ for the music of that era.

06. It's understandable that comets and eclipses from centuries ago _____ people. Scientists had yet to explain these celestial events.

07. Mark was let go for his insubordination. He was surprisingly _____ about being fired.

08. The melting of enormous Antarctic icebergs is an _____ sign of mankind's harmful impact on the Earth's environment.

09. The bully made a snide remark about the girl's dress, but she was completely _____ about the fact that he had said anything mean at all!

10. She _____ the loss of her parrot, whom she had owned since she was young.

LESSON TWENTY-SEVEN

B. Fill in the blanks in the passage with the most appropriate words.
Passage 27:

To the _____ eye, magic tricks are but a farce. However, it is easy to be _____ when a masterful magician performs tricks faster than the eye can see. It's easy to feel _____ when you see a supposedly magical trick that you cannot comprehend, but don't worry—most tricks are purposely made to be seen from _____ angles so as to make it harder to comprehend, and therefore solidify its illusory, magical quality. And besides, the audience's _____ is part of the fun!

Las Vegas, Nevada is one place where magic shows are taken very seriously. Some of the tricks are even dangerous. These _____ performances can include illusions of a woman in a box being sawed in half, a handcuffed magician being trapped in a locked glass cage full of water, and other terrifying feats of sorcery. These shows take on a fantastical, sometimes _____ air as the magicians try to make the audiences believe that something might go wrong. But don't worry—though they may seem _____, all magicians must have a certain amount of _____ or at the very least have faith in themselves to know that they can properly perform a magic trick without anything bad happening. Magic is a wonderful, exciting, often _____ kind of entertainment not recommended for the faint of heart. So keep a watchful eye and have fun next time you go to a magic show!

LESSON TWENTY-EIGHT

Target Words

1. Oppressive
2. Outraged
3. Outspoken
4. Overjoyed
5. Overwhelming
6. Pathetic
7. Patronizing
8. Passionate
9. Perplexing
10. Persuasive

A. Fill in the blanks with the most appropriate words.

01. I was _____ to learn I had passed the exam to which I had dedicated hours of studying.

02. His argument for not helping to clean the dishes was _____, and it got him nowhere.

03. Condescension is his native language. Everything he says comes across as _____.

04. The citizens were sick of being _____, so they protested against their government.

05. Her ability to _____ people into doing things for her is almost like magic. Recently she cajoled me into buying her a new laptop, and for some reason I agreed!

06. The New York Times' Sunday crossword puzzles are especially _____; I've yet to solve one.

07. People were _____ to learn that the infamous criminal had evaded justice once again.

08. Her paintings are a manifestation of her _____ for the arts.

09. American suffragettes in the early twentietht century were very _____ about wanting the right to vote, and it paid off!

10. The sheer number of bouquets and get-well cards he received while recovering from his surgery was _____ and quite touching.

LESSON TWENTY-EIGHT

B. Fill in the blanks in the passage with the most appropriate words.
Passage 28:

It was the middle of summer, and the heat was _____. The humidity was like a blanket on the entire town, _____ and inescapable, and any attempts at staying cool were rendered _____ and useless. As a result of the hot weather, people were irritable and became _____ by the smallest things. People lost their _____ for outdoor activities, and everyone wanted to stay inside. It was even hot at night, which was _____ in and of itself.

The weatherman forecast more hot weather for the next few days, which only seemed _____ to the sweltering citizens who were sick to death of the heat and humidity. But after a week, he told everyone that the heat would let up, and a cold front was moving in. People were so incredulous of this good news that the weatherman actually had to be _____ when he gave the forecast. When the cold winds at last blew through town, people were _____. Everyone's moods improved as they resumed their outdoor activities, and people were _____ about their relief that the heat wave had broken.

LESSON TWENTY-NINE

Target Words

1. Philosophical
2. Playful
3. Pleading
4. Pragmatic
5. Pretentious
6. Prodigious
7. Provocative
8. Realism
9. Reassured
10. Rebellious

A. Fill in the blanks with the most appropriate words.

01. _____ is a category of art that attempts to represent its subject matter as truthfully as possible.

02. He is the most _____ person I've ever met. Nothing is ever good enough for him, and he can always find ways to insult even the most accomplished people.

03. The puppy was especially _____ that day, so she took him out for a walk around the neighbourhood.

04. The convict's _____ did not appeal to the jury. They found him guilty.

05. I enjoy having _____ conversations about abstract concepts and theories.

06. The play was considered too _____ for young people.

07. His _____ nature was clearly a product of his terrible upbringing.

08. The meteorologist issued a tornado warning, but we were all _____ to find it was a false alarm.

09. They are very stern, _____ people. They do not enjoy whimsical movies or flights of fancy.

10. The truck can hold a _____ amount of gasoline.

LESSON TWENTY-NINE

B. Fill in the blanks in the passage with the most appropriate words.
Passage 29:

The art school professor had seen all kinds of student art projects in his time at the college. Many students created thoughtful and _____ pieces of work while others tended towards _____ or even digital art. It was common for many of the students and professors to have a somewhat _____ air about them, but the professor tried to be _____ and maintain some levity in his classroom. He was still, however, a deeply _____ man who took a _____ approach to his art classes.

It was difficult to teach art, and indeed some might argue it couldn't be taught, but he had been a part of the _____ art world long enough to know what to expect and how to conduct himself. At the beginning of each term, he encouraged his students to channel their _____ into their artwork. He also revealed that he would use a standard, traditional grading system to dole out marks, which left many students _____ that grading artwork was inconceivable. But the professor _____ them that students who worked hard, attended every class, and paid attention to his lectures would inevitably pass his class.

LESSON THIRTY

Target Words

Reflective	Resilient
Relieved	Resourceful
Reluctant	Restrained
Resentful	Restless
Resignation	Revolting

A. Fill in the blanks with the most appropriate words.

01. Her _____ to dive into the pool from the high board revealed her fear of heights.

02. They had been trying for hours to push the car out of the mud, but finally determination gave way to _____ and they just gave up.

03. I had a _____ night. I hardly slept a wink.

04. We were _____ to learn that the test results of his blood work came back negative for any deadly diseases.

05. His _____ is amazing. Once, during a power outage, he fashioned a phone charger out of lithium batteries!

06. Every employee was absent from the office that week; they were _____ against the announcement that their employer would no longer be supplying health care coverage.

07. The prisoner was a dangerous man. Whenever he had visitors, he had to be _____ in order to ensure the safety of those around him.

08. She is a deeply _____ person, almost to a fault. Often, she feels guilty about things she said or did years ago.

09. I couldn't help but feel _____ about my team's loss at the soccer game. I gave it my all, but teammates did not.

10. Marathon runners must not only be in great physical health, they must also be _____, and endure the entirety of the race.

LESSON THIRTY

B. Fill in the blanks in the passage with the most appropriate words.
Passage 30:

Rory the wrestler was _____ to hear that he had an extra week before he was supposed to compete. He _____ on his most recent competition: it had been more challenging than any before it. Rory's last opponent, a _____ and serious-faced young man his age, had beaten Rory with ease. Rory tried not to feel _____ about the embarrassing and _____ loss he had faced. Instead he tried to channel his disappointment with himself into motivation. If he thought about the loss too much, _____ about the upcoming competition was likely to set in, and that was the last thing he needed if he wanted to win!

His coach was a _____ man who came up with new tactics for Rory to try out. Though Rory was _____ to stray from his usual training schedule, he found that the new maneuvres his coach taught him could actually come in handy during the competition. The day before the competition, Rory was _____. His coach comforted him and told Rory not to be _____ during the competition—don't hold back! With the new tactics under his belt and the renewed confidence his coach had provided, Rory went into the competition optimistic about his chances of winning.

LESSON THIRTY-ONE

Target Words

Ridiculing	Scold
Righteous	Scornful
Sarcastic	Skeptical
Satirical	Sentimental
Scorching	Sensationalistic

A. Fill in the blanks with the most appropriate words.

01 The magazine alleged slanderous things about her, but she knew her reputation would not suffer. The magazine was known for being _____ and completely lacking any intellectual value.

02 The Bible claims that on Judgment Day, only the _____ will be spared.

03 The movie put a _____ spin on the common tropes found in romantic comedies.

04 My teacher _____ me for not doing the homework.

05 Ben was _____ when it came to ghosts. He did not believe in them.

06 After being endlessly _____ and beaten by the group of bullies, Tom finally took martial arts lessons so he could learn to defend himself.

07 Glassblowing is a unique line of work, though it can be dangerous. The glass is so _____ hot that if you're not careful, you can seriously burn yourself!

08 Though he claimed to have been _____, his comment hurt her feelings, nonetheless.

09 He knew his mother preferred _____ gifts to expensive ones, so he compiled old family photos and made her a scrapbook.

10 I was _____ that the towing company refused to help me, though admittedly I did not have enough money to pay them.

LESSON THIRTY-ONE

B. Fill in the blanks in the passage with the most appropriate words.
Passage 31:

The comedian was known for his _____ approach to humour. During his shows, he often made jokes about current trends and celebrities, and he was always up-to-date on what was going on in the world. He had been panned as a self-_____ jokester whose _____ style of comedy was not for the soft-hearted, but the comedian didn't care. No matter how many _____ reviews various magazines gave him, he would always feel a certain amount of _____ for such publications. In his mind, they were the _____ ones, not him!

In truth, he was actually a fairly _____ man in his everyday life offstage. His penchant for _____ everything never went home with him to his family, and the most his children ever saw of his comedic personality was an occasional _____ for bad behaviour. It was fair to say that his comedy was an extension of the darker, more _____ side of himself. He had always favoured _____ works of film, literature, and stand-up comedy, so it was no surprise that his own comedy shows were as scathing as those he enjoyed!

LESSON THIRTY-TWO

Target Words

1. Serene
2. Severe
3. Short-tempered
4. Sinister
5. Solemn
6. Sophisticated
7. Stubborn
8. Submissive
9. Superficial
10. Sympathetic

A. Fill in the blanks with the most appropriate words.

01. She painted her room blue because she'd read that the colour blue promoted _____ and positive energy.

02. He had been sullen all day, but I became extremely _____ when I learned his uncle had died.

03. The World War II movie was intense at times, and _____ at others. Many people left the theatre with tear-stained cheeks.

04. The family was known for being a _____ bunch. It didn't take much to set them off.

05. I tried to convince her that taking the highway was the fastest route, but she was _____ and took the backroads, which caused her to be late.

06. In 1950s America, it is popularly believed that housewives were taught to be _____, domesticated homemakers.

07. Teachers have no patience for students who cheat, and their punishments for doing so are _____.

08. He was a _____ man who was well read, articulate, and extremely polite.

09. The song was initially popular, but it soon came to light that the lyrics contained _____ implications.

10. He pretended to know a lot about politics, but his knowledge was _____ at best.

LESSON THIRTY-TWO

B. Fill in the blanks in the passage with the most appropriate words.
Passage 32:

The librarian was a _____ man with a _____ face and sharp, pointed features. He had often been told he always looked _____, when in reality he was only very dedicated to the library at which he had worked for over thirty years. For him, the library was a _____ environment where anyone could go to escape the _____ drama of the outside world, where low-brow entertainment like silly television shows and mind-numbing social media were favoured over _____ things like literature, history, and poetry.

The librarian ran a tight ship at the library. He assumed a _____ air when it came to people returning books on time, and could make even the most _____ library-goers pay a fine if they owed one. He was rarely _____ towards people who damaged the books, and he found that it did not do to take a _____, lenient approach towards his work. He cared for books and the library itself more than anything else, and he would protect it with his life if he had to!

LESSON THIRTY-THREE

Target Words

1. Talkative
2. Thoughtful
3. Timid
4. Toll
5. Trapped
6. Unassuming
7. Uncooperative
8. Uneasy
9. Unquestioning
10. Unselfish

A. Fill in the blanks with the most appropriate words.

01 The stray dog was _____, but we were able to lure it out with food.

02 The elevator broke down while he was in it, and for the next two hours he was _____.

03 She was afraid of the ocean, so she felt very _____ about the fact that she and her family would be going on a cruise.

04 The corrupt organization demanded _____ recruits who were willing to do anything to further their cause.

05 My overly _____ friend got us in trouble during class because the professor saw her whispering to me.

06 Mrs. Harris was moved by the _____ gift her neighbours had given her.

07 The bridge has a _____ that all drivers must pay in order to cross.

08 The _____ size of the runner was not something to underestimate. His small stature and natural thinness allowed him to run faster than everyone else.

09 He claimed his actions had been _____, but I could see that he had only done me a favour so that I might owe him one in return.

10 The employer had to fire the new intern for being _____ and not working well with others.

LESSON THIRTY-THREE

B. Fill in the blanks in the passage with the most appropriate words.
Passage 33:

Beverly was thirteen years old, and her exceedingly strict father considered her a handful. Though she was _____ when meeting new people, her _____ demeanour was only reserved for those she did not know well. With her friends, she was _____ and adventurous. Beverly loved her friends. They were _____ and _____, and they supported her _____. Sometimes Beverly's father could be mean, and if Beverly was ever _____, he would punish Beverly harshly. Her father's intermittent bouts of rage made Beverly _____, and sometimes she sneaked out of her house, in which she often felt _____ like an animal in a cage. Her father's mood swings were finally taking a _____ on Beverly, and she knew she would have to talk to the school counselor soon, before it got any worse.

LESSON THIRTY-FOUR

Target Words

1. Uplifted
2. Upstanding
3. Victorious
4. Vindictive
5. Violent
6. Virtuous
7. Whimsical
8. Witty
9. Wistful
10. Wretched

A. Fill in the blanks with the most appropriate words.

01 It was a close match, but in the end the home team was _____.

02 She considers herself more _____ than others because she does not drink alcohol.

03 A Midsummer Night's Dream is perhaps Shakespeare's most _____ play.

04 He was in a _____ state: he had been evicted from his home, he had lost his job, and his wife had filed for divorce-- all in the same week!

05 The hurricane was going to be particularly _____. People began evacuating the city.

06 I can't believe how _____ she can be! Today she put gum in my hair all because I told her I wouldn't let her copy my homework.

07 Skylar was feeling depressed, so she watched her favourite movie, which instantly _____ her spirits.

08 From aboard the ship, the naval officer waved goodbye to his wife and watched with a _____ expression as her figure grew further away until finally she was out of sight.

09 Olivia is so _____. She always has the cleverest retorts!

10 He is an _____ student who is the perfect embodiment of a humble scholar.

LESSON THIRTY-FOUR

B. Fill in the blanks in the passage with the most appropriate words.
Passage 34:

It was opening night, and Abbi was excited to perform in the play. Though she had tried out for the lead role, she had ended up being cast as a secondary character who was known for being _____ and one of the funniest characters in the play. Because of this, she felt _____ about having been cast at all. Many people had tried out, but the play was quite prestigious, and only the most _____ actors and actresses made the cut. This _____ fact made Abbi proud to be a part of the play.

Rachel, however, felt quite _____ about not being cast in the play. She had gone home after the audition in a _____ rage, and when her parents asked what was wrong, she looked at them with a _____ glint in her eyes and told them about her failure to win a role. Her parents tried to console her, saying the play was _____ and silly anyway, but Rachel couldn't help but feel jaded. Regardless, she _____ decided to go see the play on opening night because her friend Abbi had gotten a part. Rachel knew that being supportive of her friend regardless of her own irritation at not landing a role was the more _____ approach to all of this, so she set aside her anger and went to see the play.

LESSON THIRTY-FIVE

Target Words

1. Wrangle
2. Wrath
3. Wry
4. Yawn
5. Yawp
6. Yearn
7. Yelp
8. Zeal
9. Zenith
10. Zodiac

A. Fill in the blanks with the most appropriate words.

01 My mother has never much cared for astrology, but my sister is always reading about her _____ sign and corresponding horoscope.

02 It is rumoured that her _____ is a frightening thing to behold. Some go as far as to compare her fury to an erupting volcano.

03 The clothing store employee saw a customer smuggle a shirt into his bag, so she promptly ran over. The two began to _____ over whether she had the legal right to search him.

04 Her two young sons in the back seat were beginning to irritate her. They had been _____ nonstop since they had left, and she didn't know how to quiet them.

05 I detest hot weather and _____ for colder days.

06 A solar eclipse reaches its _____ when the moon completely obscures the sun.

07 They had been anticipating reading the book for over a year, and could not contain their _____ on the day it was at last released into bookstores all across the country.

08 His _____ expression gave away the fact that he had indeed been mocking me.

09 I had not slept at all the night before, so the following day I could not stop _____.

10 Cooper ran to catch the ball and let out a _____ when it hit him in the head.

LESSON THIRTY-FIVE

B. Fill in the blanks in the passage with the most appropriate words.
Passage 35:

Karen was sitting in the living room reading a book about _____ signs when her sister Jules came in. Jules sat down on the couch next to Karen and _____. They had just gotten home from school for the day and were waiting for their parents to come home. Their parents promised the girls they would take them out to dinner, so Karen and Jules had refrained from eating a big after-school snack. But now Jules was _____ to eat a substantial meal, and _____ told Karen so. Karen told her sister to quit her _____ and just wait because their parents would be home any minute. If Jules ate now, she wouldn't have an appetite for dinner and, Karen added _____, that might incur their parents' _____!

Jules became irritable and restless. She asked Karen if she could read her book, and when Karen said no, the two began to _____ over whose book it actually was! This was not how Karen was expecting to spend her afternoon. Just then, at the _____ of their argument, their parents came in. Their shocked faces said everything; both girls were in a lot of trouble!

www.ingramcontent.com/pod-product-compliance
Lightning Source LLC
Chambersburg PA
CBHW051256110526
44589CB00025B/2851